Mark Van Steenwyk

Foreword by David Fitch
Afterword by Jin Kim

the
UNkingdom
of
GOD

EMBRACING THE SUBVERSIVE
POWER OF REPENTANCE

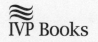

IVP Books

An imprint of InterVarsity Press
Downers Grove, Illinois

InterVarsity Press
P.O. Box 1400, Downers Grove, IL 60515-1426
World Wide Web: www.ivpress.com
Email: email@ivpress.com

InterVarsity Press® is the book-publishing division of InterVarsity Christian Fellowship/USA®, a
movement of students and faculty active on campus at hundreds of universities, colleges and schools of
nursing in the United States of America, and a member movement of the International Fellowship of
Evangelical Students. For information about local and regional activities, write Public Relations Dept.,
InterVarsity Christian Fellowship/USA, 6400 Schroeder Rd., P.O. Box 7895, Madison, WI 53707-7895,
or visit the IVCF website at www.intervarsity.org.

While all stories in this book are true, some names and identifying information in this book have been
changed to protect the privacy of the individuals involved.

Portions of chapter five are adapted from a post at themennonite.org: "Oppression is bad, now what?"
Posted September 26, 2010.

Cover design: Cindy Kiple
Interior design: Beth Hagenberg
Images: paper texture: © kevinruss/iStockphoto; praying man: © James Palmer/iStockphoto

ISBN 978-0-8308-3655-0 (print)
ISBN 978-0-8308-9567-0 (digital)

Printed in the United States of America ∞

Library of Congress Cataloging-in-Publication Data

Van Steenwyk, Mark, 1976-
  The unkingdom of God : embracing the subversive power of repentance /
  Mark Van Steenwyk.
      pages cm
  Includes bibliographical references.
  ISBN 978-0-8308-3655-0 (pbk. : alk. paper)
  1. Repentance—Christianity. 2. Christianity and culture. 3. Christian
anarchism. 4. Jesus Christ—Kingdom. I. Title.
  BT800.V36 2013
  234'.5—dc23

                                                              2013015238

P	18	17	16	15	14	13	12	11	10	9	8	7	6	5	4	3	2	1
Y	28	27	26	25	24	23	22	21	20	19	18	17	16	15	14	13			

To Jonas, my little mystic.

Contents

Foreword

When we think about anarchism, a lot of pictures come to mind: hippies, communes, idealists, protests, idiots who want to blow up everything in sight. If we're over the age of forty and have lived any meaningful years trying to meet our obligations as members of society, we look with suspicion. When we hear the qualifier *Christian* attached to the term *anarchism,* we are even more suspicious.

"This is an anomaly," we say. "Christianity is about God reconciling the world to himself in Christ and restoring the world to peace, order and righteousness. Anarchy is anything but that. Surely this cannot be Christian!" At this point in our mental processes we usually shut down.

We are tempted to dismiss it and move on.

I ask you, in writing this foreword, not to do that. Here's why:

Anarchism, Mark Van Steenwyk tells us, is the belief that "a group of people may live together without being ruled" (chapter six). We can organize our lives in ways that do not depend on coercive hierarchal authority. In doing so we gain the wherewithal to discern patterns of coercion and exploitation in our own lives and the cultural patterns we live in. We can choose to resist these things around us in the structures in which we live.

Suddenly this all sounds very Christian. If we are Christians, we should be doing this, right? Theoretically then, there is much for Christians to learn from a good anarchist like Mark Van Steenwyk.

But there is more to it than this. There is something inherently anarchist about the primary claim of Christianity: that "Jesus Christ is Lord." When we say "Jesus is Lord" we are in essence saying that God in Christ has achieved a victory over "the rulers and principalities." He now rules; no one else does. He rules over the whole world until "he has put all his enemies under his feet" (1 Cor 15:25). All other rulers, principalities and powers must become relative to that reality in our lives. Since Christ rules "not as the Gentiles do"—coercively—but in and among us with love, we too must live this way (Mk 10:42-45).

Christians, you see, in a very unique way, are anarchists. What are we to do with this? I contend that part of the answer is to read this book and become an anarchist.

"Surely you jest! How in the world are we to live like that? We have to buy a house, get a mortgage, go to grocery stores, worry about our kids' education, let the government tax us and submit to it on international relations, go use banks and let their investment professionals tell us how much money we need to retire. We have to worry about all these things. Right? How else are we to live?"

For the anarchist, the answer to all of these questions is "Not necessarily so." In fact, the Christian anarchist dares to say, "Stop everything, and discern every socio-politico-economic relationship all over again," under the terms laid down by following Christ. The Christian anarchist can help us in this basic Christian task by cracking open our imaginations to some other way.

Mark Van Steenwyk is a Christian anarchist. He can help us navigate our way through the morass of economic, social and cultural structures we must walk through each day. He may not give direct answers; instead he often just demolishes other answers. But again, don't dismiss this. This can be remarkably fruitful. I don't agree with Mark Van Steenwyk all the time. But when I do, it's life-shattering and life-changing.

Sometimes I find Mark too quick to write off the Christian participation in some political, economic or social enterprise. But when he exposes some bogus structure, some assumption that I have been using to participate in some self-protective or exploitive practice in my world, that revealing mars me forever. I am forced to repent and discern my participation in it—my own and my church's.

This is the kind of provocation the church needs at this time. Two thousand years of church history reveal many ebbs and flows to the church's ongoing relationship to culture. There have been times when the church has been persecuted and struggled for its very existence; other times the church has risen to such influence that it joined hands with the structures of society and all its powers, seeking a way to make them more just. Often in those latter times of great comfort and great power, hubris set in. Instead of subverting the empire, we got subverted by it. Every time though, down through history, God has raised up a "band of beggars" (usually at the fringes) to cry "Foul!" and expose the church's adulterous relationship with false power. From these places on the margins God has worked for the renewal of the church throughout history.

I think now is such a time. The church in North America is looking tired trying to hold onto its alignments with business, economy, university and culture. In many places, it has become too comfortable with the consumer shopping mall as its model for doing business. Sometimes I look around at the church and think its biggest need is a revolutionary manual, a manual for undoing the myths that enslave us, for revealing the ideologies that blind us, a manual that probes for new points of engagement where we can start living this grand radical life that has been made possible in Christ's victory over the powers. Mark Van Steenwyk's book could just be that manual. Christian anarchism could be the way to the fringes where God can begin anew the shaping of his people for mission.

So read on, all who dare. We cannot predict what this new anarchism will demand of our lives. But that is a good thing— maybe just what we the church need for this time and this place in our history

David E. Fitch

Introduction

Waking from the American Dream

In my senior picture, I'm wearing a red, white and blue rodeo-style shirt, a cowboy hat and cowboy boots. My nickname in high school was "Garth."

I was the only kid in town who wore a cowboy hat to school every day. There was one other kid—he was on the hockey team and had a mullet—who wore a hat to school from time to time. But he was legit; he actually rode horses. I was just a poseur. My garb was like a costume trying to communicate something: I was America.

To me, the American dream was a pure thing. James Truslow Adams coined the phrase in his book *The Epic of America*, when he referred to it as "that American dream of a better, richer, and happier life for all our citizens of every rank, which is the greatest contribution we have

The author at the age of seventeen. For those interested, the hat band is made of rattlesnake.

made to the thought and welfare of the world. That dream or hope has been present from the start. Ever since we became an independent nation, each generation has seen an uprising of ordinary Americans to save that dream from the forces which appeared to be overwhelming it."[1]

That dream meant that every citizen could achieve whatever was within their ability. It meant that all people, no matter the situation they were born into, could be free to pursue comfort and happiness without the constraint of others. And it was the job of the United States to bring that dream to the rest of the world, even if it meant fighting against those who resisted the dream.

It was this dream that made America great. It was our collective dream for all people; it was God's dream. God desired that all people could be free. Jesus died to free us from sin, and soldiers died to free us to live into the American dream. It seemed to me that God had chosen the United States of America to be his vessel for pouring out blessing upon the world.

When I was seventeen, my friends and I went to a local amusement park, Valley Fair. After a day of stuffing our faces with fried food (which I almost hurled while riding Excalibur—their largest roller coaster at the time), we settled in for the evening entertainment. They had a music extravaganza with lasers and fireworks.

The last song they played was "God Bless the USA"—perhaps the most epically patriotic song ever written. First released in 1984, it gained popularity after the Gulf War of 1990 and 1991. There was even a push to make it the national anthem. As the lasers cut patriotic images into the smoky sky, my friends and I sang our hearts out. Lee Greenwood's song is made for singing. Being a Minnesotan, I eagerly awaited the part where good ol' Lee sang about the "lakes of Minnesota," and I grew increasingly emotional as Lee sang on my behalf, "I'm proud to be an American, . . . and I'll gladly stand up next to you and defend her still today."

At this point, I could no longer sing along. With tears in my eyes and a sob in my throat, I broke down weeping. I was overwhelmed with a sense of gratitude and pride. I wept as the song played out, and I continued to weep as the fireworks began to fill the night sky. It was like a mystical experience.

I loved America. I was America.

I was optimistic about the future. Although I was youngest of six in a lower-middle-class family, I got good grades and scored well on the ACT. My plan was to join the military to pay for college and go from college to law school and then enter into politics. I dreamed of running for president in 2024.

But I wasn't just patriotic. I was devoutly Christian. I gave my life to Jesus at Bible camp when I was fourteen years old—the same summer I met my future wife, Amy. We were virgins when we married. I studied my Bible daily, wrote notes in the margins, even went to Bible college. I voted pro-life, shared the gospel with co-workers and tithed faithfully. I was the embodiment of American Christian fidelity.

It is strange how my spiritual journey has caused me to question the meaning of these words: "American Christian fidelity." In the fifteen years of our marriage, my wife and I have begun to challenge patriotism, reexamine our Christianity, and learn a very different way of being faithful together to the way of Jesus. Today, my wife, son and I live in an intentional community (which is just a fancy term for commune). We formed this community—called the Mennonite Worker (formerly Missio Dei)—in 2003. Ours is the sort of community that protests war, gets food out of dumpsters, rides bicycles, grows our own food and refers to America as an "empire." We are modern-day hippies. In high school, I would have hated me.

When I reconnect with friends from my younger years, they sometimes ask, "What happened?"

Let's go back to 1990. I was fourteen and attending a Bible camp

in rural Minnesota called Camp Joy. I was an unpopular kid in
school and was a quivering mess of insecurities around girls. If
puberty is an awkward time of life for an emerging man, then my
puberty was in puberty. To make things even more awkward, it was
high-school week, so most of the campers were older than me.

But something unexpected happened that week at camp. In the
midst of my feelings of awkward alienation, I felt connection. A
few people I met would become longtime friends, and as I mentioned above, I met my future wife that week as well. But the most
unexpected thing was what happened on the final night of camp.

It was the custom of Camp Joy to have a campfire the final evening,
right after the talent show. In those days, the fire was made down by
the lake, right next to the chapel. For many, it was the best time of
the week: fifty teenagers, gathering in a circle around a crackling
campfire as the waves of Star Lake gently slapped the shore.

The goal was to sit at the campfire with a special someone; many
new couples had formed that week. Some had already dated and
broken up. I was one of the typical campers—I wasn't dating
anyone, so I sat with friends. I had had a crush on a girl all week
but never got the courage to ask her out.

As the campfire blazed, a counselor led us in songs with a
slightly out-of-tune guitar. Between songs, campers were encouraged to share testimonies. The testifiers would walk up to the
center of the group, right in front of the fire, and tell a story about
how their lives had been changed by God. When they were done
sharing, they would pick out a stick from an old cardboard box
and throw it into the fire. It was a little ritual meant to express that
whatever was just shared was being offered up to God.

On this particular summer evening, most of the stories were
depressing. Everyone shared melancholy stories of death and dis-
appointment, of loss and regret. Several campers spoke of the
passing of a grandparent. One told about how her father used to

beat her, so she and her mother had to move away. Some told less intense stories about the death of a pet or the ending of a relationship. A few went into strangely vivid detail about past sins from which Jesus had delivered them.

In the midst of it all, I suddenly felt overwhelmed with a feeling that I had never before experienced. It was as though their pain was my pain. I felt connected to the suffering of the other campers and, even more confusing, to the suffering of the world. Nothing in my life had prepared me for that experience. It wasn't merely a feeling of empathy—it felt cosmic. It didn't feel abstract either; I felt as though I could feel the woundedness of the world. And the most painful part of that experience was that I knew, deep in the center of my being, that I was a part of that woundedness. I was broken and incomplete. And so I began to sob.

Sobbing isn't the sort of thing a fourteen-year-old is supposed to do in front of peers, particularly of the female variety. Yet there I was, weeping myself snotty in the wake of a mystical experience.

My camp counselor noticed my tears. He took me aside from the group to an old aluminum canoe about fifteen yards from the campfire. The canoe sat next to the nurses' cabin and hadn't been used in years. As we sat in the canoe, he handed me a handkerchief and asked, "Would you like to accept Jesus as your Lord and Savior?"

I didn't know what that had to do with what I was experiencing, but I assumed he knew more about these sorts of things than I did. With snotty sobs, I said yes. He then began to lead me through the "sinner's prayer."

As I look back, I regret saying yes. While I love Jesus and affirm the spiritual nature of that campfire experience, I don't believe that what I was experiencing can be described as "being convicted of sin." It was something different—something that required discernment. What I experienced was something of a conversion, but evangelicalism traditionally recognizes only one form of conversion. In following years, as I returned to camp as a counselor, I was taught to see every crisis moment, every deep spiritual experience, as an opportunity for conversion of that specific form.

That counselor was right to call me to repentance. However, he saw the call to repentance as "saying you are sorry for sin and accepting Jesus as your personal Lord and Savior." I've come to understand it differently. Repentance is, unfortunately, often understood as an event rather than a posture. But when I say "repent" I mean to turn from one direction to start walking in another. I mean that we need to start walking toward health and away from those things that bring sickness to our souls. My experience of suffering was, I believe, an invitation to engage the world differently. Such an invitation is the heart of repentance.

It wasn't the first time that my experiences would be reshaped to fit within the evangelical paradigm. When I returned home from camp, the youth leader at the church I had just started attending gave me a Bible. He told me, "start with the New Testament."

Because I was the socially awkward book-reading type, it wasn't too much of a challenge for me to dive in and read the New Testament in a couple of months. That isn't as much a testament to my intellectual aptitude as it is my lack of social skills.

An interesting challenge quickly emerged. Because I was both a fairly sophisticated reader (particularly in imaginative fiction) as well as unschooled in church superstitions, my intuitions quickly led me "astray." I assumed that the Bible was full of metaphors and poetry and prose and illustration. I didn't read it literally. Except for the parts where it was, you know, obvious. I treated the life and sermons of Jesus in a much more straightforward manner than, say, the book of Revelation or Jesus' parables.

Little did I realize that this was exactly backwards. The really obvious statements about turning the other cheek or selling your possessions were obviously *not* obvious. And the seemingly obscure and esoteric visions found in Revelation were, in fact, pretty easy to understand. Just substitute "locusts" for "helicopters" and "beast with seven heads and ten horns" with "European Union."

I didn't grasp my backwardness right away. The first inkling came during youth Sunday school on a Sunday when, later during the service, we were going to honor the veterans. (Before I continue, it may be important for you to know that I was not, at this time, anything resembling a liberal. I was living in rural Minnesota. My family was fairly conservative. My father is a Vietnam War vet. I not only fished and hunted but had my own trapline when I was in elementary school. Nothing, environmentally speaking, would have contributed to what happened next.)

During Sunday school, the youth leader asked for prayer requests. And so, head filled with recently acquired New Testament insights of a radical Jesus, I offered to pray that God would forgive our church's war vets for killing their enemies.

That didn't go over very well. The youth leader got mad. Finger-pointing-in-face mad. I was genuinely confused by his anger. I wasn't trying to cause any trouble. But I quickly learned that my way of reading the Gospels was inadequate and that my respect for my elders was insufficient.

I assumed that the mistake was on my part, so I *tried* to conform.

It took another year for the rest of my nascent radicalism to be extinguished. One occurrence stands out in my mind as the symbolic moment of that extinguishment.

I grew up near White Earth Reservation in Minnesota. Because of this, there was a higher concentration of poverty in my church than in most churches in the United States. And, especially at that time in my life, I was poor.

And so, when one of the youth workers showed up to church with a brand new, cherry red Corvette, I reacted uncharitably. After all, the economic teachings of the New Testament are fairly consistent. I couldn't conceive of any justification for someone accruing such wealth when her brothers and sisters were experiencing relative poverty. And so, I rebuked her.

"Nice car, Wendy," I said sarcastically.

She replied, "Uh . . .thanks?"

"Probably cost a lot."

I could see the suspicion grow on her face as she responded, "It wasn't too bad."

"I bet you could have fed lots of hungry kids with the amount you spent on that car," I said smugly.

I chuckle as I think back on the argument that followed. My ethical insights were pretty good, considering how new I was to the whole Christianity thing. But I had (and still have) an arrogant streak. Back then, I lacked tact. But what happened next was very much *not* funny.

Mine was a charismatic church—and not just the raise-your-hands-in-the-air kind. Ours was the cast-out-demons kind. The youth leaders set up a special prayer time for me. During that two-hour session, they tried to cast the "spirit of poverty" out of me. They also prayed for my deliverance from other spirits like the "spirit of rebellion."

My radical instincts were cast out of me like devils.

That is how I became "Garth." With my fledgling radicalism exorcised, I began to see the gospel as the animating force of the American dream. God loved me and had a wonderful, America-

Garth no more. My son and I at an "anti-fracking" protest. Jonas designed his own sign.

shaped plan for my life. The Bible was a guidebook for good, clean living.

It was a decade before I revisited those themes that seemed, in the first year of my faith, to be central to the gospel. It is odd that the things that were once considered demons, I now consider central to my faith. And the things that were once central to my faith, I now consider demonic. What was it that was cast out of me that day? And what was put in its place?

AN ODE TO PLASTIC JESUS

Entombed in plastic

My lord speaks

Brought low by thrifty men

His dangerous words forgotten

Divinity branded

His glory exchanged for a bar code

Cosmic Creator constrained

With a tiny TM

The Lion of Judah

Pushed into a cage

The Lamb of God

Sacrificed at the altar of good taste

The voice of the prophet

Silenced for profit

As affluence pours

Not to the poor

But to the affluent

In a sad twist Jesus sold at the table

Of the money changers

No one hears the cries

From inside his plastic tomb

As onward Christian soldiers

March to war

We dream an American dream

Eyes shut to the kingdom vision

Followers of Jesus shopping in the city

With Jesus bound and gagged in the trunk

A day in the life of the church

Of the American empire

One

The Gospel According
to the Empire

*Among other works well pleasing to the Divine Majesty and
cherished of our heart, this assuredly ranks highest, that in our
times especially the Catholic faith and the Christian religion be
exalted and be everywhere increased and spread, that the health
of souls be cared for and that barbarous nations be overthrown
and brought to the faith itself. . . . We [the Papacy] command
you [Spain] . . . to instruct the aforesaid inhabitants and residents and dwellers therein in the Catholic faith, and train them
in good morals.*

PAPAL BULL INTER CAETERA, *1493*

I grew up in farm country. And where there are farmers, there
are county fairs. In my early twenties, right after I got engaged
(and toward the end of my "Garth" period), I was tricked into
being an evangelist at the Becker County Fair.

Becker County takes its fair seriously, as I suspect is true in most
farming areas. Becker County is also in the heart of the lakes

country of Minnesota. Usually, the population for the county is about twenty thousand. But during the summer, with the influx of tourists, the population can triple. So, with a steady flow of farmers, locals and tourists, it was, as far as rural events go, a big deal.

One day, my friend Joe, who is a pastor in those parts, invited me to the fair. I eagerly anticipated hot dogs, fried food and the Tilt-A-Whirl.

But when we arrived, Joe turned to me and said, "Mark, I need a favor. I've got to do some errands, so I need you to work the booth."

"What booth?" I asked.

"The Heaven Booth," he replied. He had a smirk on his face.

The idea was simple. There was a booth with a big sign on the front that read: "Are you going to heaven when you die? Two-question test reveals answer!" Curious fairgoers would enter the booth, sit down and be asked the following two questions:

1. Do you think you are going to heaven when you die?

2. Why?

Every single person who entered the booth answered question one in the affirmative. However, unless they answered the second question correctly (by explaining how Jesus died on the cross for their sins), I was supposed to break it to them that they were going to burn forever in hell. Thankfully, if they were interested, I would explain to them God's plan of salvation and help them find their way to heaven. Problem solved.

At that time in my life, I was committed to the practice of evangelism; I still assumed that the best thing anyone could do was to get as many people saved as possible—that was what Jesus put us here for. But I hated every minute of it. It felt so contrived, awkward, devoid of relationship. Nevertheless, that day I led several dozen people in praying a prayer to ask Jesus into their hearts.

Early on in my shift, a beautiful young woman entered the Heaven

Booth. She was wearing a crown and a sash. She was, presumably, Miss Becker County herself. Before she entered the booth, I was already feeling socially awkward. Cold selling salvation to strangers isn't my idea of fun. When Miss Becker County entered the booth, the awkwardness became thick. Evangelizing strangers is one thing; evangelizing hot teenage strangers is another. I was overcome with a strange ambivalent combination of embarrassment, arousal, shame and piety. I was feeling shame largely because I was feeling arousal and piety at the same time. And I felt embarrassed because I was knew my face was red. Here I was, newly engaged and trying to lead people to Jesus, and I was exercising nearly superhuman will to keep my eyes focused on her face.

I don't exactly remember how she answered the two questions on the test. But I do remember that she failed. When I told her she was going to hell, she started to cry.

The only thing worse than a socially awkward twenty-year-old evangelizing an attractive beauty queen at a county fair Heaven Booth is a socially awkward twenty-year-old evangelizing a crying, attractive beauty queen at a county fair Heaven Booth.

I couldn't look her in the eyes. And I was too self-conscious to look at her anywhere else. So I remember looking to the side and muttering something like "would you like to know how you can go to heaven when you die?"

Somewhere in the midst of a snotty sniffle, she said yes. So I proceeded to explain how God sent Jesus to die for her sins, and that if she put her faith in him she'd be saved. When we were done praying together, she looked at me with a huge smile.

"I've been going to church my whole life, and nobody ever did that for me before!" she said with genuine joy. She stood up and gave me a hug. At that moment, though, I wasn't thanking God for a won soul; I was thinking of her breasts. Which led to more feelings of embarrassment, arousal, shame and (at least a little) piety.

Then she left.

I remember being relieved it was over.

But Miss Becker County soon returned . . . with every other pageant contestant. She was so filled with joy that she talked her colleagues into going to the Heaven Booth too. One by one, I awkwardly led a half-dozen beautiful young women to Jesus.

I never saw any of them again. The only record of my relationship with them was kept in my little evangelism notebook that I was asked to keep, recording a tally of souls saved.

I should have felt happy and proud that on that summer day in the late 1990s several dozen fairgoers met their Lord because of me. But the experience left me feeling confused and a little ashamed. They were little more than numbers to me that day. I objectified them all—not just the young women who left me feeling impious. Is there any great difference between a young man who keeps a tally on his bedpost and one who keeps a tally in his Bible cover? Both render something deeply intimate into a transaction. Both turn people into numbers. Both turn people into objects of conquest.

◆ ◆ ◆

Much of what passes for the propagation of the gospel actually equates to acts of oppression. When the saving of souls is of ultimate value, it can become easy for other values to be pushed aside. This evangelistic impulse turns every mystical experience into an altar call and every person into a soul to be saved. And historically Christians have shown an ability to care for people's souls while dismissing their bodies, their land or their dignity.

To many of those who have experienced oppression in the name of Jesus, Christianity has been about conquest, subduing creation, asserting its superiority over other faiths and creating a mechanism for alleviating the guilt for such unethical behavior.

Somewhere along the way, Christianity gave way to Christendom—the establishment of Christianity as a dominant cultural force, built through means that dishonor Christ. Few today celebrate those events and initiatives that secured and expanded Christendom, such as the Crusades, the Inquisition or the conquest of the New World (with its subjugation of indigenous peoples and its reliance upon slave labor). While most Christians easily recognize the sins of the past, we rarely, if ever, see how such misdeeds have any connection to our Christianity today. Usually our response to past injustices is to suggest that they have nothing to do with "real" Christianity. Should we use a gigantic time machine to transport all of today's Christians to the Crusades or the Inquisition or the conquest of the New World or the early days of American slavery, such atrocities never would have happened; "real" Christianity would win out. Christianity, therefore, remains pristine.

As we continue our march into the future, we believe that we have become better people with better societies. Perhaps we are as blind to our own complicity in injustice as the Christians in the past. One of the bad habits of Western Christianity is that it affirms the myth of progress—that the continued march of our civilization toward a better world is inevitable. It is easy to believe that the devils of our human nature live in the past—that we must simply stay the course and the world will get better, even if sociopolitical, environmental, economic and spiritual evidence suggests otherwise. This naive optimism serves to justify the sins of the past and keeps us from pursuing justice in the present.

If we want to see our past and present with open eyes, we need to remove the blinders of self-justification. To help us see our faith anew, what if we granted the oppressed the right to define Christianity? What if, that day at the Heaven Booth, I had asked the beauty contestants what they thought made a person a Christian? Perhaps it would have challenged me to be more like Christ.

Perhaps asking such questions at the macro level would help us learn why Christianity has been enmeshed within some of the most egregious examples of oppression in our world.

For two thousand years, various forms of insidious supremacy (whether it is white supremacy, national supremacy or class supremacy) have been tied with Christian supremacy—the idea that Christians are superior to non-Christians and, pushed further, that Christian culture and political structures should in some way dominate. Because Christ is sovereign, those who most represent Christ can be sovereign. The idea of the "supremacy of Christ" has been used to justify war, economic exploitation and genocide.

CHRISTIANITY IS CONQUEST

In 2010, I interviewed Dakota scholar Waziyatawin for the Iconocast podcast.[1] It was a painful interview. In it, she suggested that there is little hope that Christianity has a place in creating a just world because Christianity, at its core, is about subduing the land, asserting its dominance over people of other faiths and establishing itself as the one true religion.

Until this conversation, I had found it easy to argue against such logic. After all, that isn't what *real* Christianity is about. But in that moment, I knew that I had no place to argue. The Dakota were subjugated in the name of Christ. If the best proof I have of the goodness of Christianity is nice ideals, then my proof is worthless. Christianity is proven by deeds (isn't this what the book of James teaches?).

Waziyatawin isn't alone in believing that Christianity has no place in creating a just world, because Christianity, in the experience of so many, is about subduing the land, asserting its superiority over people of other faiths and assuming the role of the world's only true religion.

These qualities, if indeed central to Christianity, make it the ideal imperial religion. I'm sure that more than a handful of Roman emperors, European rulers and American presidents would agree.

The argument that Christianity is intrinsically oppressive is nothing new, but it persists. I believe that the dominant form of Christianity, as understood by the majority of Christians throughout the ages, is inherently oppressive and will inevitably lead to empire. There are, of course, expressions of Christianity that resist imperialism. But a Christianity that is willing to use the sword will *always* nurture empire.

At this point I should pause to explain what I mean when I use the word *empire*. Political scientists would likely define empire as what happens when one nation dominates others so that it can exploit subjugated peoples and extract the resources of subjugated lands. One people group or nation dominates other groups or nations through political, economic and military means.

In the past, empire building was rather blatant. Today, it is debated whether or not the United States functions as an empire, but with well over seven hundred military bases around the world, vast territory, economic dominance and two military occupations, it isn't difficult to make the case that it does.

Others[2] argue, however, that empire works differently in our postcolonial age. Since the mid-twentieth century, the political machines of control have been increasingly replaced with economic controls. For example, there is no need for the United States to have direct control over subordinate nations. Everyone can vote and still end up being dominated. As long as the people of the world are dependent upon our modern global economy, they remain under control without the need for military conflict. Military force is reserved for those who remain independent of our economic system (regardless of their political system). Our modern experience of globalization offers a subtle form of imperialism, where nations may seemingly exercise their own sovereignty, but the ones who shape economic realities also shape global destinies.

The global economy, the destinies of millions of the world's poor, and the resources of lands around the world are controlled by a global elite who, more than anywhere else, find their center of power in the United States of America.

But it isn't the logistical workings of empire that I want to focus on. Rather, I want to focus on the ethos of empire. How does an empire understand and justify itself? And how does the logic of empire (which is about security, domination and control) become intertwined with Christianity?

Our proximity to power and affluence gives us a strange perspective from which to read the gospel. The logic of empire is the expeditious, organized pursuit of security, prosperity and control; and the best way to ensure these things is through domination. Our entire way of life depends upon this pursuit. Yet it is contrary to the life and teachings of Jesus, who foreswore security as he walked among the marginalized and challenged the civil and religious authorities; who offered people freedom and confronted those who sought to control others; who upheld and loved the weak rather than dominating them. We find ourselves trying to justify our way of life while worshiping One who challenges our way of life.

When the way of Jesus came into direct confrontation with imperial logic, the political and religious leaders conspired to kill Jesus. And when Jesus' death didn't kill the movement, the empire found itself with a small but growing radically anti-imperial movement. The early Christians were hated by the powerful.

But things change. While it can be argued that the growth of Christianity had a positive impact on the Roman Empire, I do not believe that the inverse is true. As Christianity grew in influence, it became politically advantageous to "play nice" with Christianity. Rodney Stark suggests that in the fifty-year period between 250 and the dawn of the fourth century, Christianity grew from just over one million to over six million (out of a total population of sixty million). In other words, within about a generation, the Christian population grew from a little over 1 percent to 10 percent of the population. Within another generation, Christians came to total more than half of the Roman Empire.[3] By the time the emperor Constantine came to power in 306, Christianity was a major force in Roman society.

As Christianity gained respectfulness in the empire, its more radical tenets were downplayed. Traditionally Constantine is blamed for this shift, and for some good reasons. If you are the most powerful military leader in the history of the world, controlling vast territory and wealth, it is hard to embrace the radical teachings of Jesus. You can't fuel an empire with love of enemies. If you are trying to subjugate the world, the Sermon on the Mount makes bad foreign policy.

But the shift began before Constantine. H. A. Drake argues that as bishops grew in wealth and influence in the decades before Constantine, they grew in political power.[4] Christianity was already becoming corrupt before it was in bed with the emperor.

Traditional readings of Genesis (about subduing the land) mixed with traditional views of the lordship of Christ (giving his followers socioreligious superiority) mixed with the evangelistic impulse of the Great Commission (giving us a mandate to extend Christ's rule to the ends of the earth) are problematic enough as they stand. But if you add the willingness to use violence to accomplish these ends, you are creating the perfect empire cocktail. Before the imperial legitimization of Christianity, for example, the early church was remarkably consistent in its antiwar stance. The first known reference to Christian soldiers didn't appear until A.D. 173—long after the closing of the canon—and a Christian presence in the Roman military remained rare till the time of Constantine. After Constantine, however, the use of violence became increasingly seen as a viable way of enforcing orthodoxy.[5] A Christianity that is willing to use the sword will *always* nurture empire. If you *weaponize* the teachings of Jesus, they become imperial.

THE SUBJUGATION OF CREATION

Genesis 1:28 says, "God blessed them and said to them, 'Be fruitful and increase in number; fill the earth and subdue it. Rule over the fish in the sea and the birds in the sky and over every living creature that moves on the ground.'" Traditionally, the Christian understanding of creation sets the human being apart from nature, advocates human control of nature and implies that the natural world was created solely for our use. It continues, in the minds of many within Judeo-Christian traditions, to justify (or even compel) our deep exploitation of the earth in the name of advancing civilization. As Richard Bauckham, professor of New Testament studies at the University of St Andrews, writes: "the idea of human dominion has been the ideological justification of human domination and exploitation of nature."[6]

Genesis 1–2 has been used more than any other passage in Scripture to justify the exploitation of resources required to make empire possible. Empires require the sort of surplus and hoarding that one cannot achieve through a simple harmonious relationship with the earth; the amount of food and natural resources required to fuel armies requires that everyone in a society take more than they need to support an ever-expanding force. This was true with the Roman Empire and it is true today. Empire requires exploitation of the land.

In recent decades, Christians have embraced a model of stewardship that moves beyond themes of domination and exploitation. However, as Richard Bauckham suggests, "while stewardship avoids the themes of domination, exploitation, and re-creation that fuelled the modern project, it retains the purely vertical relationship. . . . [I]t is a limitation that suggests that the stewardship model by itself could be a perilously one-sided model for a relationship so complex as the human relationship to other creatures."[7]

As long as we see our relationship with creation in such a vertical manner, exploitation is likely to continue. As long as our needs are placed hierarchically above the needs of creation, our need to secure and safeguard ourselves in an environmentally fragile world will continue to fuel unfettered consumption of human resources. We need to learn how to practice mutual submission with creation as fellow creatures.

So while our rhetoric has shifted toward a more environmentally "aware" idea of stewardship, we continue to use the earth's resources with a primary concern for our own amusement. For example, as more in our society embrace "green capitalism"— attempting to replace consumer goods with more earth-friendly alternatives—it hasn't resulted in a slowdown of consumption overall. We are willing, when we can afford it, to use special light bulbs and buy biodegradable dish soap. But are we willing to radically simplify our lives? Few environmental scientists believe these small gestures are enough. For many Christians, the exploitation of the earth is justifiable; it is, after all, in our job description.

Historically, when a people expands in order to subdue the land, it is willing to subdue "lesser" peoples as peasant labor for agriculture and industry. While the scriptural mandate itself doesn't justify the exploitation of "lesser" nations or peoples, historian David Armitage argues that, at least within the British Empire, "God's commands to replenish the earth and assert dominion over it provided a superior right to possession for those who cultivated the land more productively than others."[8] If we embrace the subjugation of land as a divine mandate, then those who subjugate "better" have a better claim upon the land.

However, to be fair, the colonizers were probably well intentioned. Their desire was, after all, to make the subjugated more

like the subjugators, which is an attempt at coerced equality—call
it "compassionate conquest." And the compassionate conquerors
benefited as well, since they were the ones who knew how to cultivate the land to its potential. Everyone wins!

We may recoil at this logic and recognize the dark stain it has
left in the history of Western civilization. However, I believe a
version of this logic remains prevalent in our society. For example,
I know a man who paid thousands of dollars for land in Central
America, land that had recently been purchased from indigenous
people for mere hundreds. When I challenged the man on the
justice of such transactions, he replied, "those people wouldn't
know what to do with all of that money!" I have talked with many
people who justify the relative poverty of the "rest of the world"
because such people are not only less economically developed
than the so-called First World but less developed in most ways.
How far is this from the old logic of domination?

In our day, we see economic exploitation and military conquest
offered in the name of "spreading democracy" or "Third-World
development." The assumption then (and now) is that it is better
for "them" to become like "us."

I have no doubt that most modern exploitation is fueled by good
intentions. Many assume that capitalism and democracy can
nurture prosperity and freedom. The truth falls far short of good
intentions. Modern corporations—the ones that meet most of our
wants and needs—go to the ends of the earth securing natural resources for the betterment of First-World people at the expense of
locals. Look on the labels of your shirt and ask, "Would I be willing
to live like the man, woman or child who sewed this shirt?"

While modern economic exploitation is (usually) done legally,
the system intrinsically disadvantages the locals. It is the powerful that set the rules, after all. Corporations can help shape the
very laws they observe, even if the result is exploitation and op-

pression of locals. This leads to the ridiculous situation where local workers are paid mere dollars a day and a small profit from the sale of extracted resources; meanwhile, First-World people are able to gain relatively cheap goods while enjoying a comfortable standard of living.

This sort of behavior is simply a continuation of a pattern that was set by earlier Christian imperialism and colonialism. While the folks at Halliburton (one of the largest extractors of oil and natural gas in the world) probably don't quote Scriptures to justify their exploitation of natural resources and local populations, it seems that hundreds of years of a misreading of Genesis have made it possible for "good Christian folk" to support such activities as part of our larger mandate to use the world for our own purposes.

Is this the message of Genesis 1:28? Are we the lords of the earth whose divine mandate is to bring creation into subjugation? Can we assume that within the early verses of Genesis God grants us the right to farm, mine and build across the face of the earth as we see fit?

It is a mistake to assume that Genesis mandates our role as benevolent dictators of the earth. As Ched Myers points out:

> Another wordplay associates the summons to "multiply" (*rabah*) and to "rule" (*radah*). . . . [T]he primary task was to conserve the fertility of the land for the next generation—not to plunder it for short-term gain. Yet because the early Israelites were eking out a living on marginal and drought-plagued land, this task often felt like a wrestling match with the elements. It is in this sense that we should interpret the phrase "fill the land and subdue it," which has fueled modern theologies of domination.[9]

Ched Myers's interpretation is helpful because the "traditional" reading of Genesis 1:28 doesn't jibe with the way our relationship with the rest of creation is described elsewhere in Scripture. For example, in Isaiah 37:24, we read condemnation of Assyria's deforestation of old-growth cedars in Lebanon. In Ezekiel 32, the prophet decries river pollution by Pharaoh's cattle. There are limits to human stewardship that do not include domination of the land.

Another poignant example is Job 38–41 (which William Brown suggests is one of seven creation passages in the Hebrew Scriptures) in which God speaks to Job out of the storm and puts Job in his place as a part of a wild and amazing creation.[10]

The larger witness of the Hebrew Scriptures brings necessary perspective to a passage that has been used to justify the human domination of creation. Since there is a reasonably nonimperial and nonexploitative way of reading Genesis 1, it is worth asking, Why is the conventional reading so top-down? Do we believe in the human dominion of creation because it is what Scripture teaches? Or do we interpret Scripture as teaching dominion because it serves imperial interests to read it that way?

THE SUBJUGATION OF THE NATIONS

God exalted him to the highest place and gave him the name that is above every name, that at the name of Jesus every knee should bow, in heaven and on earth and under the earth, and every tongue acknowledge that Jesus Christ is Lord, to the glory of God the Father.

Philippians 2:9-11

It isn't that hard to make the leap from "my God is better than your God" to "my group is better than your group" to "my group should dominate your group." However, just because you believe in the supremacy of Christ, it doesn't *automatically* mean that you're going to dominate non-Christian groups (or groups that aren't following Christ in the best way). Or does it? If you believe that you are in the "in" group and that all others are going to hell, isn't it at least *more* likely that you'll dominate them?

The basic structures of Christianity (with some clear exceptions) make for an excellent imperial religion—you have a single God who demands that all worship him and him alone. You have a common creed. You have one church. A unified religion brought in line with a unified government is an elegant way to control the peoples. All that remains is to theologize away Jesus' ethical teachings.

Jesus calls us to give to the poor rather than save up for ourselves. Jesus teaches us to love our enemies, not bomb them to "stabilize the region." Jesus taught us to practice forgiveness, not to pursue vengeance. Jesus taught us to practice hospitality to strangers, not to live in fear of them. Jesus welcomed us into a new way of loving each other like family, not of elevating some over others.

Once notions of Jesus' care for the marginalized and his insistence on enemy-love are swept aside, it becomes easier to imagine a world in which the church and empire work in tandem to suppress non-Christian peoples in order to (1) assert the sovereignty of Christ over false gods and (2) establish Christian civilization over pagan tribes.

The superiority of Christianity over other religions has given Western imperialism the sheen of altruism for almost two thousand years. Another facet of compassionate conquest is offering the conquered a superior religion. What is temporal subjugation compared to the gift of eternal life?

It is usually assumed that religious motivation for conquest is a thing of the past—at least in the West. We take comfort that such a mindset is no longer with us . . . or is it? As I mentioned earlier, it is "democracy" rather than "Christianity" that is often articulated as the driving force of our imperialistic actions. Exceptionalism (the idea that one nation—like the United States—stands above other nations, being a beacon of hope, freedom and goodness that has a unique responsibility to nurture the world toward hope, freedom and goodness) is what drives imperialism. If a nation's interests trump the interests of other nations, then it is easier to justify the subjugation of other nations.

One cannot justify empire without somehow believing that one's own nation is superior to other nations. We justify our imperialism with our exceptionalism. How much is this superiority complex rooted in some sort of Christian exceptionalism?

I don't think our broadly Christian roots are incidental to our imperialism; they are central. The engine of Western imperialism is the quasi-Christian set of national myths that shape us into the sort of people who believe that we, uniquely, embody the good life and should spread that life to the rest of the world. The American dream is our gospel.

I will delve more into the relationship between imperialism and mythology later. However, it may be helpful to briefly explain the way in which the American dream functions as a powerful imperial myth. It is so deeply assumed in our society that middle-class existence (home ownership, college education, marriage that produces children, car ownership, disposable income and so on) is the "good life." Christianity largely exists in our society to nourish this good life. It is such a good life that almost any act is justifiable if it either (1) secures that good life for us or (2) promotes that good life among other peoples—particularly our enemies. The American dream is so deeply entrenched that it is largely unquestioned.

America serves as a brilliant example of using Christianity to reinforce empire. It is undeniable that the conquest of North America (and the conquest of the New World in general) was predicated upon Christian religious superiority. Pope Alexander VI agreed. That's why, in bull[11] *Inter caetera* he dices up Latin America between Spain and Portugal, justifying himself with these words:

Among other works well pleasing to the Divine Majesty and cherished of our heart, this assuredly ranks highest, that in our times especially the Catholic faith and the Christian religion be exalted and be everywhere increased and spread, that the health of souls be cared for and that barbarous nations be overthrown and brought to the faith itself. . . . We [the Papacy] command you [Spain] . . . to instruct the aforesaid inhabitants and residents and dwellers therein in the Catholic faith, and train them in good morals.

Such logic was repeatedly employed to justify the US conquest of North America as well (which was, after all, our Manifest Destiny). Read the words of Andrew Jackson:

The removal of the Indians beyond the limits and jurisdiction of the states does not place them beyond the reach of philanthropic aid and Christian instruction. On the contrary, those whom philanthropy or religion may induce to live among them in their new abode will be more free in the exercise of their benevolent functions than if they had remained within the limits of the states, embarrassed by their internal regulations. Now subject to no control but the superintending agency of the general government, exercised with the sole view of preserving peace, they may proceed unmolested in the interesting experiment of gradually advancing a community of American Indians from barbarism to the habits and enjoyments of civilized life.

At this point, you may be asking, "So what, Mark? It isn't Christianity's fault that America or Britain or Rome used the supremacy of Christ to legitimize empire!" Ah, but the Christianity so many of us have inherited comes to us from America or Britain or Rome. For most of us, Christianity cannot be separated from its imperial roots. Christianity isn't a set of disembodied ideas; we *learn* Christianity. And, for most of the world, Christianity is an inheritance enmeshed with imperialistic sentiments.

If we are to challenge imperialism, we must not only try to disarm the deadly idea that the supremacy of Christ legitimizes the supremacy of Christians. We must also, I believe, disarm the idea of Christ's supremacy. And we must learn from those movements and traditions within Christianity that have rejected different forms of domination.

In Philippians, Paul describes the nature of Jesus' rulership: "Who, though he was in the form of God, did not regard equality with God as something to be exploited, but emptied himself, taking the form of a slave" (Philippians 2:6-7 NRSV). Jesus' "rule" is inextricably tied to his humility and servanthood.

This isn't to say that Jesus is a humble tyrant. Rather, the very nature of his reign is humble. Roger Haydon Mitchell calls this form of rule "kenarchy," the composite of the Greek words *kenoō* (to empty) and *archō* (to rule). Mitchell writes: "Kenarchy . . . proposes that the behavior of self-emptying love . . . is the fullness of divine rule."[12] Jesus' reign isn't merely humble; he reigns through humility.

So instead of thinking of Christianity as a superior religion, wouldn't it be better to assert Christianity's inferiority? What if Christians everywhere assumed that they should take the humble jobs instead of trying to influence empire by seeking high position? The entire notion of the "supremacy" or "sovereignty" of Christ is misguided (at least if taken in a straightforward manner). Imperial language in the New Testament is largely ironic—or at the very least, redefined. To say "Jesus is Lord" is to assert that Caesar is not. And if Jesus' lordship is defined by its intrinsic humility, then what does it now mean? When we port conventional definitions for those ideas into Christ and the church, is it any wonder that we'd end up with the mess that we're in?

EVANGELISM AND CONQUEST

He said to them, "Go into all the world and preach the gospel to all creation.
Whoever believes and is baptized will be saved, but whoever does not believe
will be condemned."

Mark 16:15-16

For a majority of people throughout the ages, Christianity has been a religion of empire. It has legitimized the exploitation of creation and the subjugation of peoples. A gospel that was meant to challenge empire has become the gospel *of* empire.

So, when we speak of "evangelism" today, we are likely speaking of an imperial evangelism. Evangelism (and its well-traveled brother "missions") has been a vehicle for imperialism. This trend continues. Even the most "contextual" of ministries will often carry imperialistic thinking. Most Americans (and I assume this is true for most Westerners) are familiar enough with their own cultural embeddedness to question how much they've enculturated their understanding of their faith (to varying extents). But most Christians I know aren't as willing or able to challenge their embedded imperial context or examine their own power. It is acceptable to talk about cultural relevance in ministry, but seldom do we speak with honesty of cultural power.

And so missionaries continue to go to the ends of the earth with an understanding of the gospel that was shaped by a progressive chain of imperial contexts. And, for the most part, Christianity conformed to those contexts.

Certainly there were always pioneers who went to the ends of the earth with a message of love and mutuality. Not all of these missionaries were so deeply imperial in their thinking that they unquestioningly supported their empires. Quite the contrary.

There have always been prophetic voices like Bartolomé de Las Casas, who spoke out against oppression (mostly). But they were a small part of a larger apparatus of oppression. And rarely, if ever, were such men willing to be traitors for the cause of Christ; they spoke challenging words against oppression, but only to a point. When it came to the conquest of the New World, the Vatican was entirely complicit in colonization and conquest. While the church did seem to affirm the humanity of the natives, it was generally assumed that such natives should submit to Christian rule. To its credit, I suppose, the church's voice called for a softening of the harsher atrocities of conquest. However, it is difficult to imagine that such conquest would have happened at all without Christendom.

But you, the reader, have heard all of this before. It is ancient history. Why don't we just move on? Because we haven't repented of our gospel, and as a result we still tell the same sort of gospel. Christianity is still imperial.

Today when missionaries go to foreign lands, they are certainly more progressive. But, generally speaking, missionaries have entwined a value of modern "democracy" with their understanding of the gospel. We no longer embrace the ancient understanding of evangelism as powerlessness:

> After this the Lord appointed seventy-two others and sent them two by two ahead of him to every town and place where he was about to go. He told them, "The harvest is plentiful, but the workers are few. Ask the Lord of the harvest, therefore, to send out workers into his harvest field. Go! I am sending you out like lambs among wolves. Do not take a purse or bag or sandals; and do not greet anyone on the road." (Luke 10:1-4)

The conservatives bring a very conservative gospel filtered through centuries of Christendom. The liberals bring a social gospel that makes folks dependent upon the generosity of imperial citizens. In both cases, there is an often unrecognized power differential. It is one thing for the powerless to evangelize the powerful (read Acts). It is another thing altogether for the powerful to evangelize the relatively powerless.

This leads to all sorts of strange modern-day manifestations of the evangelism of empire. In the 1980s, there were reports of Wycliffe Bible translators being involved in funneling information to the CIA. This led to the martyrdom of Oscar Romero, Ignacio Ellacuría and others. Christian missionaries contributed to the destabilization of regions, making them more susceptible to Western interventionism. In recent years, journalists have exposed the shady activities of some within YWAM—the world's largest missions organization—trying to influence foreign governments as well as being linked to an organization called "the Family." The Family is a conservative religious organization that started the National Prayer Breakfast and has incredible access to US politicians.[13]

If you think about it, there is a sort of warped logic to imperial evangelism. If the gospel of Jesus is: "repent for the kingdom is near" then the gospel of empire is "repent for the empire is at your borders." We have replaced a gospel of liberation for one of enslavement. We have substituted the gifts of the Spirit for consumer capitalism, and mutual submission for free-market democracy.

Global evangelism often serves to prepare nations for foreign interventionism. This is true of conservative groups who link US influence with the cause of Christ, as well as progressive groups that see people of the "developing world" as objects of charity rather than the subjects of their own liberation.

To both the conservative and the progressive citizens of empire, the tendency is to bring good news to those who lack and to see the citizens of empire as liberators. This continues the old lie. Why is it that so many teenage missionaries are sent to Mexico? It is because by both conservative and liberal Christian measures, Mexicans "lack." And the more our missionaries go to such places, the more they are captivated by the imagination of empire.

Even now, in a time being heralded as "post-Christian" or at least "post-Christendom," the logic of imperial Christianity still lingers even in the most secular places. The content of the message may have changed, but the medium is still the strange messianic imperialism passed down by the Romans. And our faith is still shaped, even as Christian institutions lose influence, by imperial logic.

Two

The Powers

Mundus vult decipi, ergo decipiatur.
(The world wants to be deceived, so let it be deceived.)
PETRONIUS, FIRST CENTURY A.D.

It is bad enough that our Christianity has fueled imperialism. If the story ended there, we could simply stop contributing to the imperial machine and fix things. Christianity not only injected some of its DNA into empire (thus Christianizing it), but empire has injected its DNA into Christianity, thus imperializing our Christianity. It is nearly impossible to understand how deep the infection goes.

Ours is a faith that has largely worked in opposition to its object. Christendom has, in its imperial journey, cast out much of its anti-imperial core like demons.

Certainly there are exceptions. But they stand out as exceptions because of their rarity. There are many saints who challenged the growing imperial tendencies of our faith. St. Francis, Martin Luther King Jr., Dorothy Day, Oscar Romero . . . the list goes on. But they were in the margins. Theirs were mustard seeds of faith standing

against a growing mountain of unfaith. And I still believe that such
faith will cast that mountain into the sea.

THE PRINCIPALITIES AND POWERS

The New Testament has a strange way of talking about imperial
realities. When the book of Revelation explores the reality of imperialism, it offers apocalyptic imagery of beasts with horns and prostitutes riding dragons—things better suited for Led Zeppelin album
covers than serious conversation about modern global problems.
The apostle Paul uses language like "the principalities and powers"
to express imperial realities.[1]

It is easy to assume that things like "principalities and powers"
are either imaginary or disembodied spiritual realities, whereas
things like empires and nations are real and tangible. But, to Paul,
these were closely linked realities. In fact, he uses the same words to
describe both human structures of authority and demonic realities.[2]

The principalities and powers are social structures—social
realities—that "manage" humanity. Whenever we find ourselves
relating to one another, our Creator or our environment in a way
that is abstracted or indirect or prescribed, it is usually the result of
our participation with the principalities and powers.

In order to understand the nature of principalities and powers,
we need to explore the nature of abstraction. Abstraction is the
process by which ideas are distanced from objects. In other words,
abstraction happens when we talk about the idea of people, not the
concrete reality that is the person in front of you. Abstraction creates
layers of distance between things and people. And in some ways,
this is very useful. Some might say this is essential to being human.

Abstraction helps us step back to understand the patterns at
work in our world that can't be explained by looking at things directly. For example, it is helpful to explore poverty as an abstraction
as a way of understanding the forces that may cause a person's

material suffering. However, we run into problems if our imaginations remain abstracted.

Religion is itself an abstraction. When animated by love, religion allows us to reflect upon our relationship with God and our neighbor and the world so that we can grow deeper in our love. But religion is as likely to obscure our experience of God as to illuminate it. We can get wrapped up in beliefs and ideas and somehow remain aloof from the things those beliefs and ideas point toward. We can care about poverty but not the poor woman on the corner. We can care about the idea of love but leave it fundamentally unexpressed.

Abstraction begets evil. This is one of the assumptions I bring to the writing of this book. Abstraction keeps us from experiencing things directly. It allows us to lose individual human beings or trees or lakes or a flower in the midst of concepts like "humanity" or "nature." By abstracting war, the nightly news makes it feel like the same sort of thing as weather or sports. By abstracting complex realities of suffering and struggle, we can feel disconnected from those realities yet still somehow knowledgeable about them. There is some benefit to this—it can allow us to consider perspectives other than our own, thus helping us grow in wisdom and compassion.

Principalities and powers need abstraction to survive. And, in turn, principalities and powers keep us "stuck" in abstracted thinking so that real relationships serve the purposes of the principalities and powers. The powers and principalities work to keep us separated and alienated from one another. No wonder that when the apostle Paul tried to name "the enemy" of the gospel, he mentioned not only Satan but also these things called "principalities and powers" (see Colossians 1–2).

The only way to get otherwise good people to accept a world of war and exploitation and greed is for them to stay stuck in an abstracted way of thinking, where such things are simply "the way things are."

Where I grew up we usually thought of these "things" as generals in satanic armies. They had territories—like the principality of Minnesota or the principality of Hoboken. But reality is much more complex (and immediate) than that.

The powers aren't born in hell. They are born in the common spaces of our humanity—in the brokenness of our communities, families and relationships. They aren't born out of hate, but out of lack. They are born, not out of cruelty, but out of incomplete love.

Scripture tells us that they are created by God (Colossians 1:15-17). They started out as a creative expression of God, serving divine purposes. But they are fallen. All too easily wickedness creeps in. Greed seeps in and creates structures of economic oppression. Rage creeps in and scapegoats become victimized. Structures and ideas and systems created to help us live in harmony with one another, God and creation have become enemies to God and creation.

The powers grow in the distance that exists between God, people and the land. They are usually born to fill in the gaps, to help us reach one another and to be united. But in their fallenness they fail to bring us closer to one another. Instead they exist as layers of abstraction between us. Over time, structures meant to bring us closer to God (like formal prayer, Eucharist, Scriptures and so on) can harden and end up actually keeping people from God. Things meant to bring people together (like families) can become abusive and alienating. And structures meant to help us live in harmony with the rest of creation (like tools) can harm creation and render us unable to relate to it healthfully. This is the sad nature of the powers. They usually spring up to help us relate to each other better but become instruments of oppression.

Over time, the principalities and powers become assumed, un-contested parts of the fabric of reality. We reach the point where we cannot imagine spirituality apart from institutional religion. It seems impossible for humans to live together without things like nations. We don't know how to survive without going to the grocery store to buy things that were shipped to us from a place far away. These things are treated like necessities, yet human beings throughout history have lived without them. We no longer recognize them as abstractions. We have forgotten how to relate to God, other human beings or the land without these abstractions.

An empire is a nexus of principalities and powers—a center of massive spiritual collusion where such principalities and powers work together to serve Satan, the prince of the "world" (see Luke 4:5-7; 2 Corinthians 4:4). Walter Wink compellingly argues that the word *cosmos*—which is often translated "world" in the New Testament, should perhaps better be conceived as a "domination system." In other words, the "world" being referred to in the New Testament isn't the dirt and grass and flowers beneath our feet. It isn't nature. Rather, it is the social construct that takes place on top of that dirt—society and buildings and human interactivity.

Few human beings will willingly prefer the way of subjugation to the way of liberation. Few choose death over life. So why is it that so many participate in systems antithetical to their stated values? Much of this may be attributed to weakness or selfishness, but not all.

Sometimes folks go along with systems of death because they are forced to. But I suspect most of us in the West do so because we are clueless. This difference—between folks who participate in systems of death through coercion versus those who do so through clueless willingness is sometimes presented as the "*1984* versus *Brave New World*" systems of control.

Brave New World was written by Aldous Huxley in 1931; *1984* was written by George Orwell in 1949. Orwell and Huxley were contemporaries. They were both Englishmen, and they were both fairly progressive. While they may have agreed on what constitutes a good society, they had different concerns about social control in the modern world.

In *1984* folks are controlled overtly. The evil system of *1984* is like a stereotype of the Soviet Union, which reflects Orwell's staunch anti-Stalinist thinking. Folks know that they are being controlled but feel powerless to change their fate.

In *Brave New World*, written by Aldous Huxley in 1931, folks go along with systemic evil because they are distracted by entertainment and pleasure. They have so many choices over so much that they don't notice how they are controlled.

The evil system of *Brave New World* is like a stereotype of the United States. When folks can visit whatever websites they want, eat whatever they want and watch whatever movies they want, they don't notice the injustices that happen around the world, nor do they realize that the most important choices may not be theirs to make.

In the foreword to his classic work, *Amusing Ourselves to Death*, Neil Postman comments on the differences between Huxley's and Orwell's dystopian visions:

> Orwell feared that the truth would be concealed from us. Huxley feared the truth would be drowned in a sea of irrelevance. Orwell feared we would become a captive culture. Huxley feared we would become a trivial culture, preoccupied with some equivalent of the feelies, the orgy porgy, and the centrifugal bumblepuppy. . . . In *1984* . . . people are controlled by inflicting pain. In *Brave New World*, they are controlled by inflicting pleasure. In short, Orwell feared that what we hate will ruin us. Huxley feared that what we love will ruin us.[3]

In our "brave new world" we are bombarded by choices of enjoyments. We feel a large degree of freedom over so much of our lives that we rarely recognize how our thinking has been conditioned to accept things as they are. We accept so much injustice as simply "the way things are," and when we do notice injustices we feel so overwhelmed and fatigued by the chaos of the overloaded

"First-World" way of life that we don't know what to do about it. Usually, when someone does muster the mojo to do something about it, they use the systems already in place to address injustice, assuming that they offer the only way to remedy the world's problems. In other words, they vote. Or maybe protest. But they accept the system as it is on its own terms.

But, through the noise, most people still care about the struggle of others. They aren't so selfish that they are content to be fat and happy themselves while others suffer. But as they seek to reach out to help, their actions are often shaped by prevailing myths. Myths are the stories we internalize that help us understand how the world works. Sometimes myths are helpful. But all too often they serve the principalities and powers.

THE POWER OF MYTHS

My family moved during the summer before I began third grade. I was a shy, chubby lad in a new school. I would often retreat to the school library in those days; it was easier than trying to make friends.

I paged through hundreds of books, but I was most fascinated with mythology and folklore. One book in particular captured my imagination: *D'Aulaires' Book of Norse Myths*. The stories were good, but the illustrations were amazing. When I cracked the cover, I was transported to an enchanted world of ancient tales and epic struggle. The world of the ancient Norse was filled with fantastic creatures and giants and gods. It was much more interesting than this world—a world without myths.

Or is it? Is our modern world free from myths? Perhaps the only ones who cling to myths are religious folks who insist on believing in a Big Sky Daddy?

As I got older, the world became disenchanted. Yet our world is no less filled with myths. Ours are, perhaps, simply more boring.

Instead of three elderly Norns determining our fate, it is the invisible hand of the market.

It seems misguided to assume (as some of my atheist friends do) that to be formally "godless" is to escape the realm of myth. Myths, whether consciously linked to spiritual beliefs, shape all of our lives—no less today than in the distant past. The myths that seize us today aren't stories of gods and their quests. But with us, just as with the ancients, "myth . . . contains an element of belief, of religious belonging, of the irrational, without which it could never express what it is meant to express for [humanity]."[4] In other words, even though our myths don't outwardly resemble ancient myths, they still function in much the same way. They are the stories and symbols that give shape to our most unchallenged beliefs, that create a sense of collective belonging, that define for us what it most means to be human.

Myths become stories that we no longer question. They provide meaning and direction and shape our imaginations without us "choosing" them—they are simply "the way things are." In this way, they make the principalities and powers reasonable even when they defy logic. When myths take root in our imaginations, we can no longer imagine our lives without the myths. The most powerful myths are the ones that remain unnamed—they are taken for granted so deeply that few people ever question them.

Sometimes myths are beautiful stories and ideas that give our world a sense of wonder. Other times myths are the lies we all agree are truth. Such myths are the often untold stories that legitimize things in this world that are, themselves, illegitimate.

For good or for ill, myths are the unseen structures by which we navigate our lives. We may be able to name the powers, but how we name them and how we engage them are often determined by our guiding myths. And if the myths of our society are in service to the powers, then we find ourselves in a difficult situation.

EXPOSING FALSE MYTHS

Myths are difficult to expose. They are largely invisible. If, for example, you explain to someone that money doesn't really "exist" (except as a sort of contract printed on a piece of paper) and have value in itself, many folks will struggle to understand what you are saying. So many detrimental things in our society exist largely because no one realizes that such things need not remain. There are alternatives.

On a hot spring day in 2010, I saw several myths stripped bare. I was participating in a protest outside a government building in South Minneapolis. Hundreds had gathered to speak out against a proposed bill that would allow law enforcement to determine an individual's immigration status during any legal "stop." It would, in other words, encourage racial profiling. There were present not only a large number of Latin Americans but also allies from other backgrounds. It was, for the most part, a typical protest. Government employees furtively peeked out of their office windows while a few police officers guarded the door. The protestors held a variety of signs declaring "no one is illegal" or "this is what democracy looks like" or "love knows no borders" and so forth. Chants were chanted. Fists were raised in rhythm. Songs were sung.

It was what happened next that will forever change my way of understanding immigration. As planned, our group began to march toward Fort Snelling, where a group of Native Americans gathered.

Fort Snelling was built in the 1820s. To many, it is a quaint place to bring your family to learn about history. It is a place where middle-aged men can dress up in Civil War uniforms and reenact stuff. It is a cherished monument to the struggle of pioneers and the indomitable American spirit.

But it began as a base from which to subjugate the Dakota Nation. In the 1820s, the primary job of the military in Minnesota was to create space for white settlers. And so they built a fort overlooking the meeting of the Mississippi and Minnesota Rivers—a place where the Dakota originated. The United States government built a fort on what one could call the Dakota Garden of Eden. Aggression against the Dakota grew over the decades until the US–Dakota War of 1862. Most Dakota were driven out of the state. On November 13, 1862, about seventeen hundred of the remaining Dakota people, mostly women and children, were forcibly marched to a concentration camp at Fort Snelling. Several hundred died during the march.

On this hot spring day, Native Americans gathered at Fort Snelling to protest its existence. To them, Fort Snelling wasn't quaint. It was like Auschwitz. Yet most Minnesotans don't look at Fort Snelling with feelings of shame, but with feelings of pride.

As our group approached Fort Snelling, a group made up of Dakota and Anishinabe and others greeted us. In particular, they greeted those who are natives of the Americas.

A Dakota chief, citing tradition and treaty laws, formally welcomed all Latin American people—whether they were "legal" or not—to Minnesota. Furthermore, they were granted unconditional amnesty. The Dakota Nation had made their own immigration reform, declaring "illegal immigrants" legal. They did not grant this hospitality to the others gathered. According to the Dakota, my immigration status was questionable.

In those moments several very powerful myths were exposed:

- That the land underneath my feet is called "Minnesota" and is a part of a larger piece of land called the "United States." The indigenous peoples of this land had different ways of naming places. The idea that a political entity and the land in which that entity dwells are the same thing is amazingly counterintuitive. Yet we believe it because it is an unquestioned myth.

- That the struggle of native North Americans exists in the past. Rather, the oppression of the indigenous peoples of North

America continues. The wounds of the past haven't healed; indeed, there are fresh wounds. Most of us remain unaware of the current struggles of Native Americans because we believe the myth that such things remain in the past. Or perhaps we simply don't notice such struggles because the native population in the United States is so small (which is the result of genocidal programs on behalf of state and federal governments).

- That there is a group of people called "illegal immigrants" who need the permission of the United States government to reside in this land. Who has the right to include and exclude? By what right does the United States government set and maintain borders? In his declaration, the Dakota chief exposed the illegitimacy of the US government to declare anyone "illegal" and, furthermore, suggested that the United States was itself illegal.

No doubt, some of my readers will scoff at this example. One person's unassailable truth is another person's myth, I suppose. Nevertheless, by looking at the world through the eyes of the oppressed (as much as is possible for an educated white USAmerican man), I saw the world differently. I believe that the teaching and witness of Jesus encourages me to see the world through that lens.

It takes a lifetime of discipleship (for we are all discipled by something) to see the world in such a way that our current political realities mediate our way of seeing the world. We rarely, if ever, question the myth that there is a land—including all of its soil and rocks and lakes and wildlife—that is the United States. That story shapes our imaginations so powerfully that it is hard to see the land as itself. And there are other powerful myths that similarly mediate our relationship with the land, with the people who dwell in the land and with the God who created the land.

This is how imperial myths usually work. They cast their spell on our imaginations in such a way that injustices become part of

the "way things are." And they leave us justified in our participation in the "way things are." Even when we come to the real-
ization that they should be another way, we are left feeling impotent and unable to see a way forward.

When someone challenges the dominant myths of a society, the
empire strikes back. This happened to the prophets. It happened to
Jesus. It will happen to you, should you start poking at the myths
that hold our society together. Poke anyways; God loves us too
much for us to be enslaved by false myths.

TOWARD REPENTANCE

It isn't easy to follow Jesus with the weight of two thousand years
of imperialism in the name of Jesus bearing upon one's soul. What
are our options?

The first option is to renounce your faith. Tell yourself that it is a
problem for religious people and simply decide to become irreligious.
Or that it is a problem for Christians, and decide you are no longer a
Christian. By a simple shift in beliefs, you can have clean hands.

But what will this accomplish? By denouncing Christ do you
somehow get off the hook of empire? Does becoming an agnostic
automatically disentangle one from complicity? It is one thing to
become an agnostic or atheist out of conviction. It is quite another
to do so in an attempt to remove responsibility.

You could, I suppose, follow up such a renunciation with a bold
act of becoming an insurrectionist or a deep activist. That, to me,
is an honest way of coming to terms with empire. It makes sense
that if you choose to undo the damage of Christendom by denouncing Christ, then you must also aggressively commit yourself
to bringing healing to the legacy you've inherited. It has shaped
you; it is part of you. You weren't born with a blank slate in a world
of your own choosing. You were born into this place, and this time,
with particular privileges and histories.

The second option is willing apathy. You can let yourself grow numb and apathetic about such troubling things as modern empire, past atrocities and the continued journey toward social and environmental degradation. You can set Christianity aside as a clean ideal that helps you cope. You can embrace the imperial Christianity you've inherited. Simply tell yourself that "it isn't so bad" and that "there is nothing I can do anyway" and relax. I'm assuming that many Christians will take this option.

The third option is the most popular: simply believe that it is enough to be "aware." Tell yourself that it is enough to be aware of the problems of the world and the challenges they present to your faith, and take comfort in knowing that you are one of the few Christians who really "get it."

The fourth option is, perhaps, the least popular and most messy: you can repent of this thing we call Christianity and seek to follow Jesus. I am convinced that this is the best way forward. Jesus' way was an anti-imperial way. That is why it is so powerful as a co-opted force *for* empire.

I want to clarify something here. I am in no way advocating something as simplistic as becoming "spiritual but not religious." There is a tendency for many folks to reject the church while still affirming Jesus. There is a danger in that of simply becoming a denomination of one, with a personal deity of your own imagination that cannot be challenged by anyone else. I'm advocating a much deeper sort of repentance—one that requires deep honesty.

Our imaginations too easily fall into old patterns. We see repentance as the action of individuals. I'm not advocating that we walk away from the church and "go it alone." Rather, I believe the church needs to repent of Christianity. We must confess our sins together—to name our complicity in systems of oppression. And we need to move forward into wholeness and healing together.

Three

The Gospel of Plastic Jesus

I don't care if it rains or freezes
Long as I got my plastic Jesus.

THE GOLDCOAST SINGERS

If you want to buy Jesus, there are at least seven options available on Amazon.com. Deluxe Miracle Jesus™ is my favorite of these options. Deluxe Miracle Jesus™ comes with glow-in-the-dark hands and a water jar. You can tell it is a water jar because the mouth of the jar is blue. Flipping the jar over reveals a secret: the bottom of the jar is burgundy. Thus you can have your Deluxe Miracle Jesus™ turn water into wine. The package even includes five little plastic loaves and two plastic fishes.

Deluxe Miracle Jesus™ makes me chuckle. But somehow at the same time he makes me mad. Deluxe Miracle Jesus™ serves as a reminder of our capacity for making Jesus what we want him to be—something as tame as a plastic toy. As sacrilegious as Deluxe Miracle Jesus™ is, I find it darkly humorous that thousands of Christian parents across the United States have bought a little plastic Jesus for their children. Maybe they think that having a little toy Jesus with which to play will teach their children about the Word Made Flesh.

While little plastic Jesus can't tell us much about his older flesh-and-blood brother, he does reveal a lot about us.

JESUS OF SCANDINAVIA

The first church I ever attended regularly was in rural Minnesota. The church had that universal old-church smell—the musty odor of old carpet and dust. It was a church filled with Scandinavians. Most of the folks there had names like Johnson or Erickson. They were kind folks, but a little stoic. A little detached. Minnesotans tend toward introversion, and the people of this church were no exception.

The music served as an auditory bridge to a time long gone—a time of immigrants settling into a new land. These were the songs of the elderly—songs that they had sung for seventy years, and that their parents and grandparents had sung before them. The sermons were understated, a quiet call to a quiet faith. I can't remember a single sermon from those early days. My thirteen-year-old mind couldn't focus for fifty minutes. While I can't remember the words of those sermons, I still remember what I saw. The images reside in my memory.

The church had burgundy carpeting—not the plush kind. It was the plasticky sort of carpet that gave the worst sort of rug burn. The church had pews; almost all churches had pews in those days. The best images, however, were at the front of the church. On one side of the altar was an American flag. The other side had what was, by my best guess, a Christian flag. In the middle of it all was a picture. A picture of Jesus.

This Jesus had a soft, otherworldly glow. His eyes had a detached expression—as though he were preoccupied with heavenly truths. His sandy brown hair was soft and brushed back. His downy beard was neatly trimmed. His high forehead gently sloped downward to a strong Germanic nose. His skin was unblemished, soft and pale.

In other words, he looked like the ideal Scandinavian. This visage of Christ reflected not only a Scandinavian appearance but also a Scandinavian sensibility. This Jesus was kindly, yet detached. He was gentle, yet stoic.

It is human nature to paint Jesus in our own likeness. It is human nature to find in Jesus our highest values, our most excellent virtues.

For the past two thousand years, communities and cultures have consistently made Jesus their poster child. Sometimes, this is a good thing. After all, every culture in history has its share of praiseworthy virtues, values, beliefs and accomplishments. But every culture in history has also found new and interesting ways to suck. The problem with making Jesus into a poster child is that the ones making the poster don't always know which of their attributes are praiseworthy and which of them are damnable.

While it is human nature to paint Jesus in our own image, it is USAmerican nature to package Jesus in our own image. We don't just reimagine him. We remanufacture him. Looking into the vacant eyes of Scandinavian Jesus, I learned something about the church that mounted that Jesus at the front of their sanctuary. And I believe that I can also learn something about the church of USAmerica by looking in the little plastic eyes of Deluxe Miracle Jesus™.

THE WISDOM OF DELUXE MIRACLE JESUS™

Deluxe Miracle Jesus™ shows me that USAmericans have an uncanny ability to package everything. With profound skill, we can reduce, package, market and sell any and everything—including the divine. And while Christians throughout the ages have always shown a knack for reducing Jesus and his gospel into some handy-dandy pamphlet or doctrine, we've taken this knack to a whole new level. While Jesus has always been put into boxes, it was the rise of consumerism that created the conditions for branding, mar-

keting and selling Jesus. We have put Jesus into a little box. And
that should tell us something about ourselves.

Staring out through his plastic tomb, this plastic Jesus has a
story to tell. If the Spirit of God could animate this molded messiah
he would climb up onto my dining room table, open his little
plastic mouth and wax prophetic. He'd lift one of his glow-in-the-
dark hands palm up, as a sign of welcome. But one hand would be
thrust forward in a sign of accusation. A plastic Sermon on the
Plain. With pulsing, glowing hands cast out, maybe he would pro-
nounce something like this:

> Blessed are you who long to wake up from the American
>   dream,
> for yours is the kingdom of God.
> But woe to you who still dream the American dream,
>   for you may never wake up.
> Blessed are you who hunger for justice,
> for you will be satisfied.
> But woe to you who think things are just fine as they are,
> for you are going to end up on the outside looking in.
> Blessed are you who mourn over the church in USAmerica,
> for you will laugh when you see what I have planned for her.
> But woe to you who happily maintain the status quo,
> for you'll weep when you realize what you've done to her.
> Blessed are you who refuse to package my flesh-and-blood
>   brother,
> Who struggle to live according to his teachings,
> Even when they make you look like a hippie,
> Or un-American,
> Or just stupid.
> But woe to you who keep him in a box,
> Who have domesticated him and his teachings,

Who strive to be respectable and successful.

Normal.

Safe.

Okay, okay. Maybe I'm being a bit melodramatic. But I tell you the truth: we are guilty of far more than just manufacturing a little plastic Jesus. We're guilty of putting Jesus of Nazareth into a box. We've domesticated him. We've made him tame. We've packaged him so that he is safe for human consumption.

The fifth chapter of *The Brothers Karamazov*—called the Grand Inquisitor—contains a parable that demonstrates our tendency to domesticate Jesus. In the parable, Jesus returns during the Spanish Inquisition. The people recognize him and flock around him. He compassionately heals several of the sick and lame. Knowing who Jesus is, an elderly cardinal—the Grand Inquisitor—promptly arrests Jesus. Jesus is dangerous. He threatens the status quo. The Grand Inquisitor visits Jesus in his cell, informing him that he is no longer needed. The Inquisitor explains that Christ was wrong to reject each temptation by Satan. If Jesus had only given people what they wanted, he could have ruled. The church, which is now allied with the devil, is better able to give the people what they need. The Grand Inquisitor sets Jesus free, but banishes him. The Grand Inquisitor will continue to use the name of Jesus but has replaced his teachings for ones better equipped to meet the needs of the people. Jesus silently departs to "the dark alleys of the city."

What happens when someone who cherishes affluence encounters Jesus? What happens when the contented consumer meets Christ? One of two things—they either repent or find a way to make Jesus safe. If we're going to enjoy the fruits of the empire—if we're going to pursue the American dream, then we've got to find a way to shut Jesus up. We don't need lunatic Jesus turning over the tables of the money changers. We don't need judgmental Jesus who wilts fig trees. We don't need reckless Jesus who hangs out with unsavory people. No. Jesus exists for our fulfillment. He loves us and has a wonderful plan for our lives. And I already have an idea about what that wonderful plan is. He can help me with it if he likes.

And so, Jesus is boxed. I've mentioned that it is human nature to paint Jesus in our own image. And in an individualist society such as ours, this often means that we each have our own personalized conception of Jesus. A democrat is likely to see Jesus as an exemplar of liberal ideals. A republican might see Jesus as a moral exemplar who calls each of us to personal responsibility. Edgy urban types like me tend to see Jesus as a countercultural hero.

In our society, individualism goes hand-in-hand with consumerism. Almost everyone buys and sells things. In this sense, we're all consumers. But consumerism is a way of seeing the world, a way of life. Consumerism says we exist to consume goods, services, experiences and the pleasures of life. Everything in this world has become a product—the land beneath our feet, the people working across the street and the God who gives us life. Everyone in our society has been shaped, discipled, in the way of consumption. And as we let consumerism shape our Christianity, we go shopping for Jesus.

From there it is all about supply and demand. If enough people demand a certain version of Jesus (like a safe Jesus who exists to make me happy), then it makes sense that there will be churches that exist to supply that Jesus. A church becomes a store where folks go for their regular dose of religious goods and services—to consume Christ. In these churches, folks don't hear the gospel of Jesus Christ, they get a marketing pitch. Smart shoppers take their time to figure out which Jesus they want to believe in, and which church or ministry they ought to shop at for that ideal Jesus.

Meanwhile, people are fragmented more than ever—pulled into all sorts of directions more than ever. We are stressed and lonely and tired. We live in service to the principalities and powers. We remain blinded by our imperial myths.

The life and message of Jesus challenges this entire arrangement; encountering the living Jesus threatens the imperial order. And so, the imperial order has colluded to create a new Jesus—one that is tame. This is the Jesus in many of our churches.

Therefore, instead of offering a radically different way of life, we seem to offer yet another product to add to the shopping cart of life. Instead of knocking over the tables of money changers, Jesus is yet another product at their table. He becomes a trinket. He exists to make me happy. In other words, he is yet another tool that I can use to secure the American dream.

Four

Repenting of Christianity

"God, rid me of God."

MEISTER ECKHART

My faith collapsed with my mother's lungs.

I spent my late teens caring for my dying mother. After years of struggling with emphysema, my mom's lungs failed. Thankfully, with the help of medication and an oxygen tank, she was able to survive for the few years it took to get a lung transplant. Her surgery was successful, but the antirejection meds made her puffy, and she always seemed dangerously close to death. But she was alive . . . until she started smoking again. Within a few months of lighting up for the first time in years, she was dead. She died when I was nineteen.

During the time in life when other teenagers were getting drunk in icehouses (I wish I were making this up) or playing CB tag (if you didn't grow up in a small town before the internet existed, you wouldn't understand), I took care of my mother. The depressing nature of those years seemed to fit the spirit of the age. Gone was the optimism of the eighties, only to be replaced with the cynical honesty of the early nineties. My life read like an overwrought script about a young man's struggle with depression-laden absurdity. I was Gilbert Grape. I smelled like teen spirit.

I didn't go to college after high school, even though my ACT scores were the best of my graduating class. Family first. I didn't have many friends—a lot of my peers moved away after graduation. I was afraid to leave my mother alone. I was terrified that she would die while I was gone. In those rare occasions I'd go out with friends, my mother would shame me for staying away too long. "It is a good thing I didn't die while you were out with your friends," she would say.

My mother did let me have a part-time job. I needed money for a car and clothes, and the money she got only covered the basics: rent and food. I had what is perhaps the most soul-numbing job imaginable. I worked about fifteen hours a week sweeping a warehouse. It was a forty-thousand-square-foot freezer that housed only one thing: McDonald's french fries.

I was supposed to take a break every hour, because of the cold. I recall one time my supervisor asked me, "Why don't you ever take breaks? It is freezing in there, you're supposed to take a break sometimes."

I responded: "What's the point?"

And then I would get into my car and drive home. My car was as sad as my job. It was an old Datsun 200SX with failing breaks. It was pale blue and rusty. The driver's side seat was propped forward by a broken hard-shelled suitcase. There was no muffler, but the stereo worked.

Since my job gave me a lot of time alone to think, my mind would often ruminate over my miserable lot in life. I felt abandoned. I was the youngest of six children, yet I was left to care for my dying mother. I was a bright kid, yet I stayed in my small town while friends left for college or career. My church, which had once given my life meaning, was going through a split. I felt abandoned by family, friends and church.

I felt abandoned by God. The earlier years of my faith had been marked by deep feelings of conviction. God had seemed close to me—sometimes overwhelmingly so. But during this season, I felt nothing. Only drab loneliness.

One day, I drove home to my dying mother in my death-car after sweeping a freezer that held little slivers of frozen potato that would later get a hot oil bath and be eaten by fat faces. It was a cloudy day. This was my life.

My mother and I lived in a subsidized apartment near the trailer park on the north side of town. The walls were white, the carpet beige. I did my best to keep the apartment clean, but my mother was a hoarder. Soda cans (she drank Squirt) were strewn around the couch, my mother's nest. She had a bedroom, but she only used it for storage. She preferred the convenience of the couch—with its proximity to the television and the refrigerator—to the privacy of a bedroom.

Normally when I got home, I would go to the fridge, grab a soda and proceed to sit down in my chair to watch television with my mother. It was the closest thing to bonding I had with her; we watched *Days of Our Lives* together.

But on this day I only mumbled to her as I walked directly to my room. Earlier, as I swept dust off of a cold concrete floor, I had reflected upon my sad life and decided that I would formally renounce Christ.

I wanted to do it properly. I cleared space in the middle of my bedroom floor. I stripped naked and lay down upon the beige carpet of my bedroom, eyes staring up at the ceiling. After a time of silence, I began speaking words of rejection to God, committing intentional acts of blasphemy. If God had forsaken me, I would forsake God.

I'll spare you all of the blasphemous details. I blasphemed, forsook and unprayed for about an hour. When it was over, I was tired and numb; there was no release. No closure. I was just a naked, depressed teenager lying on the floor.

But then, in the silence, something happened. I felt the presence of Christ. It wasn't accompanied by joy; it was accompanied with deeper feelings of sadness. In my soul, I knew that this deepening sadness was not my own, but the sorrow of Christ. Christ had come to commiserate. In those moments I knew he felt as I felt. He seemed as fed up, as angry, as depressed. He was with me in the midst of my grey season.

As I lay in silent sadness, Jesus said: "Let it all go. Forsake it all. But you can't forsake me, because I haven't abandoned you. You can reject everything—the church, your theology, everything, but I'm still here." And then things drifted back to normal. I was left on the floor in silent sadness.

My life continued in the same sad way, but something small had shifted. I look back upon that day as the reason I'm a Christian. By forsaking Christ, I found Christ. Or, to be more precise, he found me.

EVERYTHING THAT IS NOT GOD

In recent years, I've begun reading the works of French activist, mystic and philosopher Simone Weil. She's one of those intellectuals that is often quoted but rarely read. She defies easy categorization. A third of the time, I am struck with her brilliance. During the other two thirds, I alternate between feelings of active boredom and mental irritation. I'd like to share with you one of her brilliant (yet irritating) statements. I share it because it speaks to my experience of failed apostasy:

> It is not for man to seek, or even to believe in God. He has only to refuse to believe in everything that is not God.

This refusal does not presuppose belief. It is enough to recognize, what is obvious to any mind, that all the goods of this world, past, present, or future, real or imaginary, are finite and limited and radically incapable of satisfying the desire which burns perpetually within us for an infinite and perfect good. . . . It is not a matter of self-questioning or searching. A man has only to persist in his refusal, and one day or another God will come to him.[1]

That day, when I yelled at the ceiling in defiance, was the first time it had ever occurred to me that the Christ of my imagination might bear little to no resemblance to the living Christ. This was—and still is—an unsettling notion. But I have become comfortable with being unsettled. That is, I believe, the nature of faith.

Our notions of God are often the biggest obstacles to knowing God. For much of my life, my Christianity has been a string of idolatrous ideas that have separated me from Christ—ideas that keep the untamed God safely distant.

I have come to know Christ in the letting go of Christ. My prayer has become the same as thirteenth-century mystic Meister Eckhart's: "God, rid me of God."

God is found in the letting go of God. We cannot cling to God. Rather, we find that God clings to us. In our clinging, we continue to insist that God exist in a particular way and do particular things. This makes God our slave and, as a result, we remain enslaved to our God-thoughts.

So much of my Christianity (and I believe the historic expression of Christianity over the past two thousand years) has been an attempt to keep Christ in a cage. We don't want a free, living Christ—one who we cannot control.

We treat the living Jesus like a doddering fool, humored to his face yet secretly disdained. The dead Jesus, who has never lived, is our god. This dead Jesus is a compilation and distillation of our self-serving ideals. We gladly worship this Jesus, since he is a personification of our most apparent desires and dreams—desires and dreams that have been shaped by our shared myths.

If we want to follow Christ, we need to repent of our Christianity. Granted, there is no such "thing" as Christianity—Christianity has always been a messy constellation of ideas and traditions. Even the apostles Peter and Paul disagreed over what it was all about (for example, see Galatians 2). And things have only gotten more complicated. Today, it is impossible to speak of a single thing called "Christianity" since it is a fluid and flexible social grouping of over a billion people who rarely, if ever, fit into any textbook definitions. While this thing we try to call "Christianity" is really a huge messy pile of constantly changing ideas and traditions, few (if any) of those ideas and traditions remain untainted from the stain of domination.

So, when I say "Christianity" I am referring generally to the dominant strands of Christianity that make up the bulk of the Western tradition. In particular, my experience is primarily with Protestant Christianity in America. I grew up in Minnesota among Lutherans, came to faith among charismatics and Pentecostals, came of age among nondenominational evangelicals, went to seminary with Baptists, began to ask questions with Emergents and became a pastor among Mennonites. And while I don't claim to be an expert on any of these traditions, I believe that the challenges and encouragements of this book apply to each—and more.

For two millennia we Christians have been complicit in the deepest sins of Western civilization. No doubt, Christianity has contributed to our triumphs as well. As I read history, I find countless stories that inspire me to become a more loving human being. But few would disagree that the historical reality of Christianity falls far short of our ideals. Given the wide gap by which we have collectively fallen short, one must question whether or not our stated ideals are the ones we actually hold.

This gap is problematic. Christianity is a religion that places embodiment at the center. Ours isn't a religion of disembodied ideals but of flesh-and-blood realities. Whatever we are in practice is what we value most in our hearts. If, as Paul suggests in 2 Corinthians 3, our lives are to be like living epistles from Christ, what happens when we more closely resemble a horror story? Or at best, a dark comedy? Who then is our author?

Why is that when critics point out the ugly story of Christian domination, so many Christians argue that those examples aren't *real* Christianity? That when self-described Christians commit genocide, oppress the poor, subjugate women or simply act wickedly, they aren't *real* Christians; their actions have nothing to do with their alleged faith.

And so, successive generations of Christians can avoid responsibility. We can distance ourselves from the sins of the past without having to examine whether or not the same genocidal/racist/sexist/classist tendencies are embedded within the fabric of our own Christianity.

I'm fairly certain that Jesus' vision wasn't to leave us nifty ideals in a book. His vision wasn't a set of disembodied doctrines. Rather, it is something we live out. And if the majority of the ways it has been lived out have been enmeshed with a history of domination or oppression, then that is the Christian witness to the world. Yes, we can all point to some glorious idea in a book and say that is the real Christianity, but what good does that do anybody?

So while there may be a disembodied, completely pure definition of Christianity that exists as some sort of platonic ideal, the closest thing to such Christianity is rarely (if ever) seen in the real world. Our task should be less about defining an ever-purer utopian Christianity and more about embodying a tangible way of love.

And so, we find ourselves with a dilemma. Most of us can point to a loving ideal—a disembodied utopia of Christianity—but for most people throughout history Christianity has been complicit in bringing injustice. The most public and prolific examples of Christianity in our world today are in opposition to our ideals.

Jesus has become a tool of empire. Those who conquer often adopt the mythologies of the conquered; it allows them to maintain status quo even as they open controlled spaces for folks to speak of revolution. Whether we like it or not, even radical Christian stories have been appropriated into the mythologies of Western civilization. We live in a society where the largest military machine in the history of the world can erect a monument to Dr. King. We live in a world where a president can name Jesus Christ as his favorite philosopher and, shortly thereafter, launch two wars.

Our ways of understanding liberation, freedom, goodness, prosperity and happiness have largely been shaped by the American dream (or its other national variations). The ways that Christianity has been corrupted as a tool to captivate our imaginations in service of Western civilization run deep.

THREE WAYS OF OPTING OUT

Repenting of our Christianity, however, isn't as easy as simply "opting out." Over the past several years, I've met a number of people who, when they realize the dark history of Christendom, simply walk away from Christianity, sometimes in the belief that their de-conversion gets them off the hook for sins perpetrated in the name of Jesus Christ. While I respect that some honestly migrate away from Christianity, I don't believe it is intellectually honest to opt out as a way of removing shame; one doesn't need to be a professing Christian to have had their imagination shaped by Christendom. Even though I didn't embrace Christianity until my teens, I have been shaped by Christian ideas and stories (though it would be more precise to call them quasi-Christian USAmerican imperialism narratives) my whole life. We are shaped not only by the stories of Christendom, we have learned to think and act and feel by Christendom.

There is another way folks try to opt out; by laying claim to a more radical Christianity, many foolishly assume that they've changed sides. They jump from team "Empire" to team "Radical." This is very much akin to a white dude somehow claiming he is, in fact, no longer a racist after taking a college course addressing racism (or participating in a racial reconciliation workshop). I've identified myself as a "radical" Christian for about ten years. At no point has my racism or sexism or classism magically disappeared. It doesn't work that way. Racism and sexism and classism aren't positions people hold; they're lenses through which we see the world. So even if you suddenly change your mind, it takes a lifetime to change your lens.

In their effort to change sides, some attempt to opt out of their complicity in Christian imperialism by joining a more radical form of Christianity. This was part of my own rationale for joining the Mennonites. But Mennonites, despite a relationship to empire that is relatively unique among Christians, are still shaped adversely by Christendom. For example, while most Mennonites reject violence, few Mennonites challenge economic exploitation. And even that commitment to nonviolence is eroding over time. Furthermore, to speak personally, joining a pacifist tradition didn't magically eradicate the violence in my own heart. Escaping to a more radical Christianity in and of itself is not a solution to our complicity in an imperial form of Christianity.

A third way of opting out is more subtle. If the three responses to a threat are "flight, fight or freeze" (the previous two options being flight and fight), then the freeze response is simply to be crushed by a mountain of shame. I want to spend a bit more time discussing this response because I believe it is the most pervasive way of opting out.

Shame is anger turned inward. It can even become self-hatred. And, usually, that self-anger comes from a mixture of lies and truth. We have all internalized lies that cause us to hate ourselves. But shame can also stem from being confronted with a hard truth.

For example, many men I know feel a particular sense of shame around sex. I'm the same way. Deep inside, part of me believes that sex is dirty, that it is wrong. I believe this because so much in our society reinforces this—from the way media depicts sex as "transgressive" or "naughty" to the way television shows men to be pigs who "only think of one thing." Moreover, many of the messages we hear from our churches about sex (when sex is actually talked about) further enhance both our confusion and the association between sex and shame.[2] Because of this, I have to struggle as a married man with a tendency to view sexual longings and urges as shameful and wrong.

When one holds such a secret shame that is based upon lies, it is hard to hear the truth. The truth about the complexities of sexuality and the goodness of sexual desire is hard for me to really embrace. It is also hard for me to hear the truth about the high percentage of men who can be sexually abusive or unfaithful. Speaking truth to the lies doesn't necessarily lead to liberation. At first, it just heightened my experience of shame.

Another example can be seen at a national level. We all know, at least superficially, of the dark history of the United States. Most of us, to some degree, feel shame about that. Indeed, I have some internalized anger over the privileges I get in this society simply by virtue of being a heterosexual white man.

It is true: the villains who enslaved and subjugated are long dead. Yet, they are convenient scapegoats. When I look at this nation, I see some of the fruits of that oppression, and I have more access to enjoy those fruits. I feel ashamed. The shame comes from the truth that I am complicit in continuing the legacy of oppression, even if that complicity isn't active. But the lie that contributes to that shame is that "this is just the way it is" or that "justice is impossible" or even "white men don't have a role to play in seeking justice."

Repentance isn't dwelling on shame. It is working through the shame. By confessing the truth while rejecting lies we can begin to see a way forward. By confessing the goodness of sex while rejecting the lie that sex is dirty, I can learn how to worship God and love my wife with a liberated sexuality. By confessing the dark history of my society and the painful truth of my present privilege while, at the same time, continuing to learn my role in seeking justice, I can find true joy rather than a false joy based upon avoidance of the truth. When we work through shame, it becomes revolutionary.

It would seem that our society has become expert at avoiding shame rather than working through shame. When we can name that shame, recognize our internalized anger and direct the anger at its most appropriate target, we can create space for liberation. Anger at ourselves for inaction can spur us toward action in the future. Anger at a system that marginalizes people and steals their voices can move us to tearing that system down.

When avoidance of shame becomes pathology, we demonize truth tellers. This is why Israel killed its prophets. It is why we kill ours (or imprison or ostracize them). Let us listen to the voices coming to us from the wilderness, calling us to repentance.

Feeling shame is an invitation to repentance. It is a recognition that something is wrong that manifests as self-anger. If we can open up space to examine that shame, talk about that shame and confess that shame, we are on the path of repentance. And when we collectively repent as our response to collective shame, we are on the path to revolution.

The roots of empire go deep. Learning a new script takes a
lifetime. If I am going to be faithful to the way of Jesus (which is
tricky, since my understanding of Jesus and his way has been so
shaped by oppressive systems), I need to confess the brokenness of
my Christianity in full recognition of how much it has shaped my
identity. It is, for better or worse, part of who I am.

So I don't think it is honest to "opt out" by simply rejecting
Christianity (that's about like washing the outside of a cup but
leaving the inside dirty) or joining some radical Christian enclave
(as if such a thing actually existed) or simply going numb as a response to crushing shame (which serves no positive purpose what-
soever). Instead, we need to repent of Christianity.

Repentance is not an event or an emotion, it is an ongoing invitation to engage the world differently—to see the world the way
God does and act accordingly. Repenting of Christianity means
adopting a posture of honest confession as we seek a better way.

A story is told about a respected scholar who leaves his university to pursue enlightenment. Eventually, he visits the home of
a renowned Zen master.

"Please, master, I have come to find enlightenment," he says as
the master answers his door. The master welcomes him and, as a
good host, offers the scholar some tea.

They sit. The master begins pouring tea into the scholar's cup.
Once the cup is full, he keeps pouring until it overflows. He keeps
pouring as it spills onto the table and onto the floor.

At this, the scholar exclaims: "the cup is overflowing; you can't
pour any more into it!" The master replies, "Like this cup, you are
overflowing with your own ideas. How can I show you enlightenment if you are already full?"

We think we are open to learning the way of Jesus, but our cup
is already full of our own ideas. Unfortunately, we don't notice
that it is full. As a result, many of us can spend our lives pouring

sermons and Scripture readings into our minds, but they simply spill back out. At best, we simply baptize our own thoughts and suggest that they are Jesus' thoughts. Our lives are full to the brim with societal myths. The stories read to us as children, the toys we played with, the television we've watched, the books we've read, the advertisements we've absorbed, the laws we've followed—all of these have shaped us. And now our minds can't even imagine the alternatives.

We need to empty our cups. We need to repent of the myths that crowd our imaginations. We need to repent of our Christianity.

Gelassenheit is a German word from the medieval mystics. For some, it was a sort of inner quiet that led to detachment from worldly concerns. But for others, particularly the Anabaptists, *Gelassenheit* was practical. *Gelassenheit* isn't simply about an individual's inner spiritual life but is about relationships with others.

Gelassenheit is about ridding one's life of all obstacles to love of God and neighbor. As the early Anabaptist Hans Haffner wrote in his devotional tract *Concerning a True Soldier of Christ*: "When we truly realize the love of God we will be ready to give up ["give up" is an English translation of *Gelassenheit*] for love's sake even what God has given us."[3] Love is the one thing that remains because, while love often feels like an abstraction, it is the most real. John taught that "God is love" (1 John 4:8). Paul taught that everything will pass away, but faith, hope and love will remain—and the greatest of these is love (1 Corinthians 13:13). Jesus said that the Law and the Prophets all hang on our love of God and neighbor (Matthew 22:34-40).

When I say we need to repent of Christianity, I am advocating that we let go of beliefs and structures and institutions and buildings and money and stories—everything that we put upon Jesus—and ask "Is this the way of love?" or "Is this separating me from God and my neighbor?"

What we need now, more than ever, is a new spirituality of *Gelassenheit*, one that seeks to remove all of the obstacles to our love. One that understands the intrinsic relationship between love of God and love of others. A spirituality that will gladly set aside all things—even if they are a gift of God—for love's sake.

This isn't to say that we should embrace a simplistic, naive spirituality devoid of stories and structures. I'm simply advocating that we recognize them as abstractions that must be yielded to God. Otherwise they will become the idols we worship in place of God.

I need to repent of Christianity in order to love God and neighbor. But I cannot repent of it by simply walking away—it is a part of me. And so, I cannot repent of Christianity without naming myself as a Christian.

I am a Christian; I repent of Christianity. This is my religion. I will keep saying that for the rest of my life. The moment I stop yielding my Christianity to God is the moment I stop loving.

If we attempt to bring about social justice without a life of repentance, we will presumptuously carry our imperialism with us into the margins. When empire enters the margins, it is usually considered "colonization." If we are going to be agents of God's love, we have to yield our hearts to God for decolonization. This is, painfully, a lifelong process. I don't assume that I'll ever be free from subtly colonizing habits and attitudes. And I certainly won't ever entirely escape from the social privileges afforded to me by virtue of my status as an educated, white, USAmerican male. Nevertheless, out of love for God and neighbor, everything—even my Christianity—needs to yield.

Gelassenheit is a spirituality for those of us who follow Jesus in the empire. Apart from such a spirituality, we are either left with dogmatism on the one hand or Marxist materialism (the idea that we simply need to attend to human structures in our quest for justice) on the other. The former clings so much that it remains willfully unable to embrace liberation. The latter assumes that it has moved past Christianity (when, in reality, often such folks are merely evangelical Marxists).

But in all things, may we give up for love's sake even what God has given us.

My favorite novel, *Silence*, follows a Portuguese priest, Rodrigues, on a dangerous mission to Japan (during the Tokugawa shogunate). Rodrigues is sent to investigate the growing number of faithful who are apostatizing, particularly Father Ferreira, a famous missionary. After a time in Japan, Rodrigues is (through the deceit of a friend) turned in to authorities.

Rodrigues holds to a triumphant European Christ. In his faithfulness, he clings to Jesus even amidst torture. He continues in his steadfastness as apostate Christians are tortured in front of him. He remains pure even as everyone else forsakes Christ.

But the stakes are raised; he is told that if he doesn't forsake Christ by stepping on a fumie (which is an image of the crucified Christ) many of the apostate Christians will be killed. Does he cling faithfully to the Christ of the fumie, or does he forsake him, therein saving others? In this act he is confronted with an entirely different understanding of Christ, whose voice speaks after a long silence:

> The first rays of the dawn appear. The light shines on his long neck stretched out like a chicken and upon the bony shoulders. The priest grasps the fumie with both hands bringing it close to his eyes. He would like to press to his own face that face trampled on by so many feet. With saddened glance he stares intently at the man in the centre of the fumie, worn down and hollow with the constant trampling. A tear is about to fall from his eye. "Ah," he says trembling, "the pain!"
>   . . . The priest raises his foot. In it he feels a dull, heavy

pain. This is no mere formality. He will now trample on what he has considered the most beautiful thing in his life, on what he has believed most pure, on what is filled with the ideals and dreams of man. How his foot aches! And then the Christ in bronze speaks to the priest: "Trample! Trample! I more than anyone know of the pain in your foot. Trample! It was to be trampled on by men that I was born into this world. It was to share men's pain that I carried my cross."

The priest placed his foot on the fumie. Dawn broke. And far in the distance the cock crew.[4]

Are we willing to forsake our image of Christ in order to become as Christ? Are we willing to repent of our Christianity in order to be the love of Christ in our world?

Five

On the Mysticism of Children

*Truly I tell you, unless you change and become
like little children, you will never enter
the kingdom of heaven.*

Matthew 18:3

One late December afternoon, I stood with my wife and my son
Jonas—then three-and-a-half years old—in line at a cheap all-
you-can-eat Asian buffet restaurant. Like most buffet restaurants,
the food was both enticing and disgusting at the same time. This
particular restaurant boasts the largest seating capacity in Minneapolis. The convergence of cheap food, wide selection and ample
seating makes it a convenient choice for parents looking for a no-
hassle approach to feeding their kids. I'm not alone in this opinion;
about a third of the diners during this particular visit were kids.
Predictably, most of these kids seemed heavier than average.

As I stood in line, I felt the sort of guilt that is unique to parents.
It is that feeling that comes when one realizes, "If I keep doing this,

I'm going to ruin my kid." Nevertheless, on this occasion (as often happens with parents), my desire for convenience trumped my dull pangs of guilt. And so we stayed in line, slowly inching forward, waiting to be seated as my wife, Amy, went off to the bathroom.

Near the entrance was an entirely-too-large water fountain—clearly an attempt to "class things up." Jonas wanted to throw a penny in. When Amy got back from the bathroom, she held our place in line while Jonas and I went to the cheesy plastic-rock fountain. I had two pennies in my pocket. Jonas jumped up and down with excitement as I placed them in his eager hand. Still caught up in the excitement, he threw them both in at the same time. My son has never been the sort of kid to draw out enjoyable experiences.

"What did you wish for?" I asked.

Jonas scrunched up his face a little. That's his "thinking face."

I added: "It's ok if you forgot. The wish still counts if you can come up with one before wish-time runs out." I was, of course, bending the truth about wish protocol.

Almost immediately, his face unscrunched. He looked into my eyes. "That Jesus could be alive," he said.

His answer surprised me. I had told him the usual Bible stories: that Jesus was born in a manger, that he healed people and told us to love each other and that he died. But I had always stressed that Jesus rose up from the dead, that he was alive now and that someday he would come for everyone who has died (like grandma Gloria or great-grandma Mildred) and give them new life.

I began to worry that someone was trying to undo my attempts to shape my son's theology. I started mentally rounding up suspects in my mind.

"But Jonas, Jesus IS alive!" I said with joyful certainty. I thought he would nod, the way children sometimes do when you remind them of things they have forgotten. But his response shook me. I remember it often.

"Jesus is dead in the buildings and in the cities and in the outside. But he is alive in our hearts."

And then he skipped away to stand next to his mommy in line.

◆   ◆   ◆

I have no idea what my son was thinking. Little kids say silly things; sometimes those silly things sound wise. Perhaps there is wisdom in silliness. Nevertheless, his statement went straight to my heart. In that moment, I was struck with the conviction that if Jesus doesn't dwell in my own heart, I will not see him anywhere else. If I claim that Jesus lives, then he must live in me.

Upon hearing this story, a friend directed me to a quote from medieval German mystic Meister Eckhart. It affirmed and echoed the words of my son: "We are celebrating the feast of the Eternal Birth which God the Father has borne and never ceases to bear in all eternity. . . . But if it takes not place in me, what avails it? Everything lies in this, that it should take place in me."[1]

We can condemn the brokenness of the world around us. We can long for a new world—one full and complete and happy. But if the seed of that new world is not in us—if it is not in me—what hope do we have? Jesus is dead if he is not alive in our hearts.

Perhaps my son Jonas is a little mystic. Or perhaps he, like all children, makes strange, unexpected connections between words and ideas.

Little kids tend to use words like they use blocks—in ways that seem abstract, disorganized. They show you something that looks like modern art—angular, with discordant colors—and happily proclaim: "Look, Daddy, a pirate ship!"

Such emerging imaginations are often stifled and constrained by social convention. By the time they enter elementary school, children have learned that pirate ships are brown, that they float in blue water and that they are, well, boat-shaped. To an extent, this imaginative conformity is good. Children need to learn how to navigate the world in ways that keep them safe, respectful to other people and patient in the face of challenges. The job of parents and guardians is helping them focus on those things that are good while helping them say no to those things that are bad or harmful.

But there is a downside to this conformity. Not all of our social conventions are wise or true. As we grow, our pirate-ship aesthetics aren't the only things that get shaped by our society. What once was an imaginative possibility becomes an impossibility. This is okay when the imaginative possibility is being able to reach the moon by climbing a tree. But it is disastrous when we disregard other childish notions: like the belief that everyone should be able to live in a home or the belief that coins are just shiny toys or that boundaries on maps are just pretend (all things my son Jonas believes). We have to learn that not everyone can have a place to live or that money has value or that there is a place called the United States that is governed by a small percentage of predominantly white men in a place far away. Let's be honest: Which perspective is truer?

The mind of the child is largely unconstrained. They have eyes to see the world in ways that their parents no longer can. Children aren't stifled with shame or guilt or propriety or politeness. They have to *learn* those things (usually from their parents). They are feral, and we domesticate them.[2] Often this domestication enslaves their minds and hearts to ideas that render them unable to experience the fullness of the world.

In many important ways, children see the world around them more truly than their parents. They see the world with an unfettered imagination. Within our spiritual tradition, such unfettering is the province of the prophets and the mystics.

The prophets have an imagination for what the world *could* be. They remind us that things don't have to be as they are. The mystics see the world differently; they see a reality that others miss. The prophet exposes lies while the mystic reveals the truth. Both are required for liberation.

Traditionally, mysticism is defined as having an unmediated encounter with the divine. Mystics live in a world where the veil between heaven and earth is extremely thin. All of the layers between the mystic and God are stripped away and the mystic experiences God's presence.

The stripping away of layers—the collapsing of spiritual distance—can happen in all kinds of ways. Some mystics encounter God alone in their room. But others experience the presence of God in the face of a stranger. Still others encounter God in nature. In all of these experiences, mysticism isn't otherworldly. It is about encountering the living God wherever God may be. Mysticism collapses the distance between a person and God, between people, and between a person and the rest of creation. At its best, mysticism points toward a life free from abstraction, where you simply see what is.

Because of this, many mystical movements have been on the forefront of social justice. Mystics often see beyond the myths of their society and, in refusing the power of those myths, are able to embody lives of justice. The French mystic and philosopher Simone Weil once wrote: "Truth is too dangerous to touch, it is an explosive."[3] Perhaps this is why mystics have often been ostracized, existing in the margins either by force or by choice. Their experiences threaten to invalidate or destroy the structures and layers that the establishment clings to for its survival. So, when I use the word *mystic*, I mean "those people who see the world with spiritual eyes and, therefore, see things for what they truly are."

There is a danger in walking the path of the prophet apart from that of the mystic. If we attempt to transform the world around us without a renewed imagination, we are likely to repeat the cycle of injustice in fresh ways. There is a danger in walking the path of the mystic apart from that of the prophet as well: that we will move inward without attending to the injustices around us.

Through the eyes of my son, I see the world differently. But I also recognize that the world as it is need not be his inheritance.

Children live in worlds as large as their imaginations. And so, unfortunately, do adults. Our problem is not simply that our world is a broken place. Our problem is also that we live in too small of a world, where our imaginations cannot see a way forward. We accept "what is" all too readily.

When Jesus says, "Truly I tell you, anyone who will not receive the kingdom of God like a little child will never enter it" (Mark 10:15), he is likely talking about the need for disciples to embrace the vulnerable posture of children, to be in solidarity with the most weak in society. But I often wonder if, perhaps, Jesus also understood that the naive, innocent minds of children are uniquely able to believe in divine impossibilities like the kingdom of God.

If we are going to enter the kingdom of God, we need to have childlike imaginations. Our way of seeing the world perpetuates what we see in the world. If we accept the dehumanizing, dominating, destructive patterns of our world as "the way things are" we cannot help but reinforce those patterns.

If children are mystics, then mysticism is not the domain of a detached, esoteric elite. Rather, mysticism is for all of us. The unexpected collapsing of the distances between God, human beings and the rest of creation is something all can experience. For many, mystical experiences are rare. As Dorothee Sölle suggests, "By banishing [mystical experiences] from our children, we destroy them within ourselves at the same moment."[4] We live in a world free from mystical possibilities because we do not nurture them in our children. Nor do we recognize them in our communities. We have built a prison free from wonder.

Yet there is hope. Sölle writes: "When we start digging up the buried mysticism of childhood, the feeling of oneness and of being overcome arises anew. Memory clings to little, insignificant details."[5] In my own experiences, the ability to see the world through God's eyes begins with remembering childhood moments when wonder was a regular part of my life. By remembering my childhood, I am free to regain the faith of a child.

When we, like children, see the glimpses of the real world—where distance between people, the land and the Creator is collapsed; where things like money or governments or class superiority are understood to be collaborative lies—we are getting close to the practice of *naming*.

Radical educator Paulo Freire suggests that naming is the heart of what it means to be authentically human:

> To exist, humanly, is to *name* the world, to change it. Once named, the world in its turn reappears to the namers as a problem and requires of them a new *naming*. . . . But while to say the true word—which is work, which is praxis—is to transform the world, saying that word is not the privilege of some few persons, but the right of everyone. Consequently, no one can say a true word alone—nor can she say it *for* another, in a prescriptive act which robs others of their words. . . . The naming of the world, which is an act of creation and re-creation, is not possible if it is not infused with love.[6]

What does this naming look like? It is noticing when members of the dominant culture are the only ones speaking in a mixed group and pointing it out. It is confessing those times when we've dismissed people because of our unintentional prejudices. It is acknowledging the dignity and beauty of those experiencing injustice. It is standing with societal castoffs while denouncing the systems that disregard them.

Naming happens whenever truth is spoken in the face of untruth and is acted upon. It is risky.

Naming happens when we bring hidden things to light, speak truth in the midst of error or confess our complicity in systems that devalue others. Naming is about loosing the lies and binding the reality with our attentiveness, presence, words and actions. We are moving beyond mere symbolism to real praxis—acting in a way that unveils the oppression and cocreates liberation.

For example, we once had a man, "Malcolm," apply for long-term residence at the Mennonite Worker. Before a new housemate moves into one of our community houses, the members of the community have to reach consensus. In this particular case, it took us months to reach consensus. Since Malcolm was in his sixties, had significant health issues and had disabilities, we reached a unanimous decision to reject his application. A process that lasted months was finally over.

All that week, I felt troubled by the decision. So much prayer and discussion had been involved and we had finally reached consensus (those of you who have engaged in consensus decision making understand how difficult it can be). Yet, I felt like we had made a mistake. I felt as though our decision had been driven by anxiety, not upon the leading of the Spirit. And so, one week after reaching full consensus, I awkwardly monkey-wrenched the endeavor.

"I know we reached consensus . . . so I can't block consensus anymore, but if I could go back to last week and do so, I would," I said as I awkwardly avoided eye contact with members of my community. I went on to explain how I felt I had been making decisions based upon anxiety and that I hadn't completely valued what Malcolm brought to our community—I was fixated on his age and health and disabilities. I was, in other words, making decisions like an anxious snob, and I suspected that the Spirit might be saying something different.

The reaction surprised me: I heard sighs of relief. Within ten minutes we reached consensus to overturn a decision that had taken months to make. I named my anxiety. I named my ageism (my bias against Malcolm because of his age) and ableism (my bias against Malcolm's disabilities). By bringing these hidden things to light, we were able to include someone who would otherwise be excluded. And, as a result, not only was Malcolm's life changed, ours were as well.

Naming is what Jesus was doing in the Sermon on the Mount. In the Beatitudes, Jesus is naming the truth and opening the space for a new reality in that naming. Were the poor blessed before Jesus said "blessed are the poor"?

Were they, as we've assumed, blessed because of their awareness of need? Was Jesus sentimentalizing? Or was he, in that moment of naming, unveiling the lies, and, with his fellow poor, cocreating a new reality? A new moment where previously entrenched realities break open so that a new future is possible? This is revolution-speak.

In the existing order, the wealthy and powerful and privileged were insiders. The poor were outsiders. In the Sermon on the Mount, Jesus flipped the social arrangement by naming the excluded as part of the blessed. It was, in effect, like saying, "We don't need that system of power and inclusion. . . . Here and now, *we* can be the community God desires."

Naming is about the in-breaking of God. When we speak the truth in the midst of a system of lies, the truth becomes planted like a seed. And as we continue naming, that truth begins to grow. In the Christian tradition, naming is almost the same thing as proclaiming the gospel.

Later, on our way home, I wanted Jonas to tell Mommy what he had told me at the fountain. I'm one of those parents who likes to show off the intelligence of his kid. Unfortunately, Jonas never repeats himself; I can never get him to repeat his clever stories or phrases. I think Jonas enjoys subverting me.

"Jonas," I asked, "is Jesus alive?"

This time, he answered: "Jesus is everywhere, but he is alive in our hearts."

"But earlier you said he was dead in the cities and buildings and in the outside!" I retorted.

He replied, "He is dead in those places because Herod tried to kill him and the bad people killed him and put him on a cross."

Jonas sees no contradiction between Jesus being dead in some places but alive everywhere. Of course, this isn't a rational idea, but it is, perhaps, a true one. In every moment, in every place, it is possible to encounter God—to see the world made new, to name the truth and push back lies. But, it is also true that there are places and moments of de-creation—where death reigns.

I'm reminded of the words of Ignacio Ellacuría, who was martyred in El Salvador in 1989:

> Among the signs that are always appearing, some striking and others barely perceptible, there is an outstanding one in every age, in whose light all the others must be discerned and interpreted. That sign is always the historically crucified people, which remains constant although the historical forms of crucifixion are different. That people is the historical continuation of the servant of Yahweh, whose humanity is still being disfigured by the sin of the world.[7]

Where oppression reigns, people experience death. But where oppression reigns, Christ is suffering with the people. And where Christ encounters death, there is the possibility of resurrection.

Jesus is dead in the places we kill him. But he lives in our hearts. In each moment we're pulled in two directions—to continue to live in the broken world-as-it-is or to name the world, recreating it as the kingdom of God breaks in.

In this way, the Great Commission to "go and make disciples of all nations" is a mandate for naming. The Great Commission can be seen as a top-down task of proselytizing or expanding Christendom. Or it can be seen as a bottom-up task of liberation. I am reminded of these stirring words by the immensely underappreciated William Stringfellow:

> The premise of most urban church work, it seems, is that in order for the Church to minister among the poor, the Church has to be rich, that is, to have specially trained personnel, huge budgets, many facilities, rummage to distribute, and a whole battery of social services. Rather, the opposite is the case. The Church must be free to be poor in order to minister among the poor. The Church must trust the Gospel enough to come among the poor with nothing to offer the poor except the Gospel, except the power to discern and the courage to expose the Gospel as it is already mediated in the life of the poor. . . . When the Church has the freedom itself to be poor among the poor, it will know how to use what riches it has. When the Church has that freedom, it will know also how to minister among the rich and powerful. When the Church has that freedom, it will be a missionary people again in all the world.[8]

The kingdom of God breaks into our reality through the lives of the seemingly insignificant. In small acts. In true words. We don't experience God's presence in the places of power or wealth or prestige. The kingdom comes to us in the unexpected places.

It won't begin unless it begins within us. Jesus is everywhere.

His presence in-breaks and sustains. But he is dead in the places where he isn't animated by the hearts of his people. We cannot change in the world what isn't true with us. Let us reclaim the imagination of children and enter the kingdom. Let us show the world Jesus' impossible vision.

Six

Jesus and
the Unkingdom

*That holy anarchist who summoned the people at the bottom,
the outcasts and "sinners," the chandalas within Judaism, to
opposition against the dominant order . . . was a political
criminal. . . . This brought him to the cross.*

FRIEDRICH NIETZSCHE

As we see in the Gospels, Christ's kingship is inconsistent with
traditional structures of power; and for this reason, Jesus tells
Pilate that "My kingdom is not from this world" (John 18:36
NRSV). Passages like these have, unfortunately, fostered an inef-
fectual otherworldliness among Christians. And they have been
used to legitimate "real-world" kingdoms. Jesus rules some
magical sky-kingdom, while princes and emperors can dominate
flesh and land.

Traditional kingship (with absolute power, hoards of wealth and
power over the weak) has nothing to do with Jesus; it's something
Jesus rejected (see John 6:15).

Traditional kings demand allegiance and servitude, but Jesus offers liberation—from suffering, sickness and death, exclusion, persecution and sin. Jesus is a "king" who serves the "least of these" and who finally receives torture and execution to bring freedom to others.

But Jesus' reign isn't otherworldly. It isn't apolitical. It's just political in a radically different way. Rather than taking Caesar's throne (or any throne—including the one Satan offered him; see Matthew 4:1-11; Luke 4:1-13), Jesus is saying that Caesar's days are numbered. By saying "my kingdom is not from this world" he isn't saying "my kingdom is only spiritual, so you don't have to worry." A number of scholars have successfully made this point. For example, N. T. Wright argues,

> The sentence should not be read as referring to an otherworldly, Platonic, non-physical kingdom. It designates Jesus' kingdom as the breaking into the worldly order of a rule which comes from elsewhere, from Israel's God, the creator God. It does not mean the abandonment of the created order and the escape into a private or "spiritual" sphere. On to the scene of worldly power—precisely there, or it is meaningless!—has come a new order of sovereignty, which wins its victories by a new method.[1]

Jesus' kingship renders Caesar's obsolete. It isn't a mere "trumping" as though Jesus is simply *greater* than Caesar; it is an entirely different sort of kingship.

As heirs to Jesus' kingdom, we are ambassadors of the new reign, privileged to share the mercy, love, peace and justice of Christ with the world. In the early days—the first century of the Jesus movement—the church was invisible to most people in the Roman Empire. However, they had a growing reputation as an alternative and seemingly antisocial community that lived in the nooks and crannies of empire.

So, when Jesus said his kingdom wasn't of this world, he wasn't understood by Pilate or by the Jews or by his earliest followers as talking about the afterlife or some abstracted spiritual truth. Based upon the lethal response to Jesus (and the early reactions to Jesus' movement), the "kingdom of God" was understood as a challenge to Caesar and his reign. Their two kingdoms clashed.

The kingdom of God that Jesus announced and embodied is what life would be like on earth, here and now, if God were king and the rulers of this world were not. Imagine if God ruled the nations.

But in order to imagine that, we'd need to recognize that Jesus' kingdom isn't the sort that one holds with an iron fist. Despite our images of God, I'm not sure that God is interested in either hierarchy or control. For where the president of the United States insists on a troop surge, Jesus calls people to love their enemies. Where dictators seek to secure their own power and prestige, Jesus calls people to serve one another and lay down their lives for friends. Since Jesus is (as Christians believe) the truest revelation of God, then he defines for us what the reign of God looks like.

The social, economic, political and religious subversions of such an unreign are almost endless—peacemaking instead of warmongering, liberation not exploitation, sacrifice rather than subjugation, mercy not vengeance, care for the vulnerable instead of privileges for the powerful, generosity instead of greed, embrace rather than exclusion.

It is radically insufficient to simply say that Jesus' authority trumps other sorts of authority. This assumes that Jesus is just *more* kingly than earthly rulers, or that Jesus is just more powerful than the global elite. There is truth in this. But it is perhaps more apt to see Jesus' authority as so counter to earthly authority that it is, in fact, an unauthority. And authority to end authority. His power is a subversive power that tears down the elite. It tears down mountains and lifts up valleys.

Jesus is calling for a loving anarchy. An unkingdom. Of which he is the unking.[2]

NAMERS OF ALL FORMS OF OPPRESSION

Defining anarchism is problematic (to "define" something often implies the authority to do so, after all). Nevertheless, for the sake of clarity, I will offer my best attempt at a reasonable definition. *Anarch* means contrary to authority or without ruler. So *anarchism* is the name given to the idea that a group of people may live together without being ruled.

That is the textbook definition. Most anarchists go further, trying to name and resist all the things in our societies that oppress people. Elisabeth Schüssler Fiorenza coined the helpful term *kyriarchy* (from the Greek word *kyrios*, which can signify the domination of the emperor, lord, master, father, husband or elite propertied male) to signify the complex interrelatedness of various forms of oppression (like classism, sexism, racism and so on). These various forms of domination do not stand alone. Rather, they reinforce one another into a domination system.[3]

I have found it helpful to focus my critique on the "empire" as a manifestation of interrelated oppressions. Empire is, in our context, that social reality (or unreality, depending upon how you look at it) that globally reaches out to manage all of creation (including humanity) into a system of exploitation wherein only the elite ultimately benefit.

Empire is the bringing of death to the whole of life. Good anarchists are namers of all forms of oppression, seeking to understand the way oppressions reinforce each other in enslaving creation and seeing, in contrast, a way of liberation and life for all of creation.

Anarchism is, as a defined idea, a new concept. This complicates any effort to delve too deeply into the past in order to name any group or movement as "anarchist." However, as anthropologist David Graeber writes:

> The basic principles of anarchism—self-organization, voluntary association, mutual aid—referred to forms of human behavior . . . have been around about as long as humanity. The same goes for the rejection of the State and of all forms of structural violence, inequality, or domination . . . even the assumption that all these forms are somehow related and reinforce each other. None of it was presented as some startling new doctrine. And in fact it was not: one can find records of people making similar arguments throughout history, despite the fact there is every reason to believe that in most times and places, such opinions were the ones least likely to be written down. We are talking less about a body of theory, then, than about an attitude, or perhaps one might even say a faith: the rejection of certain types of social relations, the confidence that certain others would be much better ones on which to build a livable society, the belief that such a society could actually exist.[4]

It would make sense for those who follow Jesus Christ (who presumably want to embody the way of love) to feel drawn to a set of practices that seek to remove oppressive social relations and, instead, seek a new way of relating. Christians can learn from anarchists.

ANARCHIC IMPULSES IN SCRIPTURE

A superficial reading of the Bible reveals a God who thinks of himself as a sort of Warrior King, who sanctions state-enacted genocide and who promotes a string of saintly kings, like King David. Many Christians assume that when Jesus arrives, it is to start a kingdom of God that, apparently, seems content to coexist with earthly rulership. They hear Jesus saying "render to Caesar what is Caesar's" and Paul advocating being good subjects to the governing authorities. Therefore, Christian anarchism can be seen as a contradiction in terms.

Furthermore, how can Christian anarchists hold views like non-violence when many biblical heroes were prolific smiters? How can Christian anarchists support communal ownership when certain patriarchs were "blessed" with vast property—which they didn't share equally with all? How can Christian anarchists argue for consensus decision making when Paul tends to affirm male leadership and Jesus praises a centurion who holds a position of authority? To many people, the last thing the Bible offers is an anarchist perspective.

I think there is a different way to read Scripture. There is an anarchic impulse running throughout Scripture that, once you find it, begins to subvert many conventional interpretations.

THE HEBREW SCRIPTURES

Let's start at the beginning. Genesis can be read as an anti-civilizational text. It begins with the story of humans living in harmony with nature and upholds that as a pristine ideal.

As Ched Myers suggests,

> in the "primeval history" of Gen 1–11 Israel's sages—re-dacting older sources and probably writing in the aftermath of the failed monarchy—also attempted to explain [the rupture from primal life]. Eden can be interpreted as a mythic memory of the old symbiotic lifeways: humans, creatures and God dwell intimately and richly together (Gen 2).[5]

When paradise is lost, humans are relegated to hard agricultural toil. The first act of violence is committed by the agriculturalist (Cain) rather than the nomadic herdsman (Abel). It is this murderer who establishes the first city. Later, as humanity "progresses" all sorts of crazy things happen, like when the human population spikes, the "sons of *elohim*" have sex with women, people become increasingly wicked and God sends a flood to reboot creation. Later, when folks gather to build a huge tower that reaches to the heavens, God scatters the people. For the most part, Genesis is remarkably negative about the way wickedness increases with the march of civilization.

Again, Myers writes:

> The "Fall" in Gen 1–11, then, is not so much a cosmic moment of moral failure as it is a progressive "history" of decline into civilization—exactly contrary to the Myth of Progress. The biblical primeval history thus should be considered not only as "mythic memory," but also perhaps the first literature of resistance to the grand project of civilization—rightly warning against its social pathologies and ecocidal consequences.[6]

The rest of Genesis follows the story of the first patriarchs, who YHWH has called out to become a people who will follow YHWH into a Promised Land. Throughout Genesis, trouble happens when the Jews favorably interact with imperial powers or try to settle too soon. While it is true that the patriarchs had many possessions, it is a stretch to infer from their wealth modern notions of property rights. Preagricultural nomadic peoples were tribal. While the patriarchs were hardly egalitarian, their understanding of ownership was much more communal than modern Western notions. The wealth of the tribe or clan or family was for the benefit of all.

Exodus tells the story of a people enslaved by the Egyptian Empire and how YHWH delivers them. You know the story: YHWH calls Moses (in the burning-bush theophany) to lead the Israelites out of slavery into a Promised Land. Of course, once they are lib-

erated, the people grumble and complain, desiring a return to
Egypt instead of the long journey in the wilderness. In Exodus we
see a "story of Israel's communal bonding around the mountain
at which they encounter YHWH, with no need for 'sacrifice' of
animals or enemies."[7] As a result of their grumbling, YHWH keeps
them in the wilderness for forty years.

Then, apparently, Moses passes the mantle of leadership to
Joshua—a sort of military hero who engages in war against the indigenous peoples of Canaan.[8] The people successfully settle and
are attacked by their neighbors, leading YHWH to raise up "judges"
to lead the people in combat against the enemies of Israel.

YHWH sets up a brilliant economic policy centered around the
sabbath. Every seven days was a day of rest, every seven years was
a time for the land to rest, and every seven times seven years was
the Jubilee, when all slaves were set free, every debt was released
and even the land reverted back to its ancestral ownership. It was
an economic system that condemned usury, struck the root of
generational poverty and condemned the exploitation of foreigners.

YHWH also instituted a strange political system; instead of
having a centralized government, temporary leaders were called as
need arose. Instead of a king, God dwelled among the people to
rule directly rather than ruling through kings or priests. For example, one of the leaders who emerges, Gideon, tells the people, "I
will not rule over you, nor will my son rule over you. The LORD
will rule over you" (Judges 8:23). Unfortunately, Gideon's offspring
attempt to set up a dynasty.

But the people complained for a king, and eventually YHWH
relented. Saul—who fit the people's idea of a king—was a failure.
After he died in battle, David (after some oft-told Bible stories tran-
spire) became king. The kingdom split during the time of David's
grandson. Conflicts between the prophets and the kings became
commonplace as Israel became increasingly like its neighbors,

leading to the eventual demise and captivity of both the northern and southern kingdoms.

This story—from Exodus to the monarchy—is one of centralization and waywardness. As Wes Howard-Brook writes,

> As it stands in its canonical order, the story conveys a relatively (and deceivingly) simple message: the shift from a twelve tribe confederacy under YHWH's rule to a human monarchy "like the nations" (1 Sam 8:5) was a disastrous betrayal of the unique status of Israel as YHWH's "chosen people." . . . Israel "converted" from a religion of creation to the religion of empire, with predictable results.[9]

It is important to highlight some of what makes this a "deceivingly" simple message. It is simplistic (and foolish) to assume that the days of David and Solomon, with a monarchy centralized in Jerusalem and worship centralized in a temple in Zion, should be considered a golden age. There is, according to Howard-Brook, a tension (or outright contradiction) between the promonarchic "'Zion theology' that placed YHWH in the Jerusalem temple" where Solomon "could be understood as truly empowered by YHWH with 'wisdom'" and the prophetic "Sinai theology" where "Solomon's 'experience' can be written off as either wishful thinking or simply as propaganda."[10]

In other words, the Hebrew Scriptures present a sort of argument between the religion of *empire* (where a faithful, powerful, secure, wealthy and vast nation is centralized in Jerusalem, where YHWH and king dwell) and the religion of *creation* (where a faithful people live in Jubilee, encounter YHWH in creation and amidst people, and live as kin without an earthly ruler).

As we read through the Prophets, when God speaks, it is usually through a prophet who challenges the king's power and who stands outside of the machines of the monarchy. The emphases of the kings are very different than those of the prophets. It is astonishing how much the prophets link idolatry and exploitation of the poor. The kings often centralize wealth and power. The prophets challenge that trend. The prophets, it would seem, still hold God's Jubilee vision in their imaginations.

Ezekiel 34 points to a time when God will rescue Israel from captivity and bring things back to God's original intent: the "shepherds" or rulers over Israel will be struck down, and God will become shepherd.

> For this is what the Sovereign LORD says: I myself will search for my sheep and look after them. . . . I myself will tend my sheep and have them lie down, declares the Sovereign LORD. I will search for the lost and bring back the strays. I will bind up the injured and strengthen the weak, but the sleek and the strong I will destroy. I will shepherd the flock with justice. (Ezekiel 34:11, 15-16)

THE NEW TESTAMENT

If Wes Howard-Brook is right about there being an argument in Scripture between the religion of empire and the religion of creation, then Jesus clearly and consistently sides with the religion of creation.

Jesus' mother, while Jesus was still in the womb, said the following words while filled with the Spirit:

> [God] has demonstrated power with [God's] arm; [God] has scattered those whose pride wells up from the sheer arrogance of their hearts. [God] has brought down the mighty from their thrones, and has lifted up those of lowly position; [God] has filled the hungry with good things, and has sent the rich away empty. (Luke 1:51-53 NET)

Jesus grows up. He starts his ministry and is tempted by the devil in the wilderness. The temptation of Jesus by the devil reveals the manner in which Jesus understands his authority. Jesus' sense of authority bears little to no similarity to kingly authority. In the wilderness, he is tempted politically, economically and religiously to assert his messiahship. But he refuses. The diabolical nature of his temptation isn't due to the source of the temptation—the fact that the offer of political, economic and religious power comes from the devil instead of God. Rather, the temptation concerns the sort of reign Jesus should pursue.[11] Jesus is the unking.

Later in Luke 4, right after his trial and baptism, Jesus goes to his hometown (Nazareth) and gives a political manifesto of liberation for the poor and oppressed, essentially announcing his messiahship and the coming of Jubilee[12] (the "year of the Lord's favor"). Provocatively, Jesus seems willing to include oppressors in the kingdom. The context makes this clear. The miracles Jesus references in his sermon involve the healing of Gentiles. Furthermore, when quoting Isaiah 61, he omits the portion that speaks of "the day of vengeance of our God," which was understood to refer to vengeance against the Gentile oppressors of Israel. This is why his hometown folks— who most likely knew him well—try to kill him.[13]

In Luke 17:21 Jesus quotes Leo Tolstoy[14]: "The kingdom of God is within you" (or "among you" or "in your midst"). In this context, it seems to be a way of suggesting that the kingdom of God isn't a place, a demonstrative regime change or a clear event. Rather it is here. Now. Jesus didn't like the way the political game was played, so he played a different sort of game altogether: one where there needn't be losers.

Later, when Jesus heard his friends arguing amongst themselves the pecking order in this kingdom, he tells them: "The kings of the Gentiles lord it over them; and those who exercise authority over them call themselves Benefactors. But you are not to be like that. Instead, the greatest among you should be like the youngest, and the one who rules like the one who serves" (Luke 22:25-26). Jesus is asking his friends to rethink everything they know about sociopolitical realities.

The next time you read the Gospel of Luke, try to read it through the lens of Jubilee—where the ones who have accumulated have to give up their wealth and the ones who have lost receive.[15] Jesus tells the rich young ruler to sell everything and give it to the poor (Luke 18:18-30). He says the same thing to his disciples, by the way (Luke 12:13-34).[16]

Luke isn't the only anarchist-friendly Gospel; John is also pretty juicy. For example, Jesus calls Satan "the prince of the world" (see John 12:31, 14:30, 16:11)—which is likely a way of referring to the Roman Empire. The word we translate as "world" is *kosmos*, which Walter Wink establishes as meaning something closer to "domination system" or "empire."[17]

After the resurrection, we read of an account of civil disobedience in Acts 5. When the disciples are ordered by authorities to stop their teaching, they answer: "We must obey God rather than any human authority (NLT)." Here's what most people have been taught this means: "We must obey God rather than any human authority in those rare circumstances where there is a clear and obvious contradiction between what the law says and God says, since God's laws trump human laws." I'm not so sure. If you believed that your messiah was a sociopolitical/religious unking who died and then rose from the dead (and then mystically poured his Spirit out upon you), then you might simply mean "we must obey God, not any human authority."

This helps us understand the way in which the early church practiced community. They were encouraged, among other things, to work out their issues internally rather than appealing to the courts (1 Corinthians 6:1-6). In Romans 12:2 (NET), Paul argues that his friends in Rome should "not be conformed to this present world [read: empire], but be transformed by the renewing of your mind, so that you may test and approve what is the will of God." This is often read as a call to be spiritually minded. But, given the larger context, it is perhaps better to see it as a challenge to stop being so Roman-ish and instead pursue the way of love. I am often asked to justify my anti-imperial reading of the New Testament. After all, the word *empire* doesn't appear in the New Testament. Well. Here's the thing. The early church was sneaky. They didn't want to sound overtly treasonous. So usually we have to try to inhabit their context with our imaginations to see Rome closer to the way they saw it. And no writing is as anti-imperial as, perhaps, John's Revelation.

The "Babylon" referred to throughout Revelation was Rome: the ancient seat of imperial power during the days of exile (Babylon) came to signify the current imperial power. As Wes Howard-Brook and Anthony Gwyther argue, Revelation isn't a challenge to Roman imperialism in particular, but against imperialism in general. Rome was the face of an old enemy.[18]

Babylon is described as "a dwelling for demons and a haunt for every impure spirit, . . . for all the nations have drunk the maddening wine of her adulteries. The kings of the earth committed adultery with her, and the merchants of the earth grew rich from her excessive luxuries" (Revelation 18:2-3). In response to imperialism, a voice from heaven declares: "Come out of her, my people, so that you will not share in her sins" (Revelation 18:4).

BUT WHAT ABOUT . . . ?

We read Scripture in ways that support authoritarianism because we learned how to read Scripture in authoritarian contexts. Once you start pulling the loose threads, you begin to find the whole authoritarian fabric unraveling. For sake of brevity, I'll address the two most commonly raised passages against Christian anarchism.

What about "submit to the governing authorities"? The first is
Romans 13, where Paul tells his readers to "submit to the governing authorities":

> Let everyone be subject to the governing authorities, for there
> is no authority except that which God has established. The au-
> thorities that exist have been established by God. Consequently,
> whoever rebels against the authority is rebelling against what
> God has instituted, and those who do so will bring judgment
> on themselves. For rulers hold no terror for those who do right,
> but for those who do wrong. Do you want to be free from fear
> of the one in authority? Then do what is right and you will be
> commended. For the one in authority is God's servant for your
> good. But if you do wrong, be afraid, for rulers do not bear the
> sword for no reason. They are God's servants, agents of wrath
> to bring punishment on the wrongdoer. Therefore, it is nec-
> essary to submit to the authorities, not only because of possible
> punishment but also as a matter of conscience.
>
> This is also why you pay taxes, for the authorities are
> God's servants, who give their full time to governing. Give to
> everyone what you owe: If you owe taxes, pay taxes; if
> revenue, then revenue; if respect, then respect; if honor, then
> honor. (Romans 13:1-7)

When interpreting this passage, there are several things that one
must keep in mind:

This passage occurs immediately after Romans 12, where Paul
challenges his readers to bless persecutors, live peaceably, never
avenge, feed enemies and overcome evil with good. By implication,
the "governing authorities" are enemies who've been persecuting
the Christians and whose evil needs to be overcome with good.
Given that Paul is likely drawing directly from Jesus' teachings, it
may be best to interpret the call to "be subject" as an application of

the call to "turn the other cheek." It is not a call to mere obedience or happy citizenship.

Not only is the passage a call to turn the other cheek, but it is also a recognition that conventional wisdom would be to strike back. Jacques Ellul suggests "the passage thus counsels nonrevolution, but in so doing, by that very fact, it also teaches the intrinsic nonlegitimacy of institutions."[19] In other words, the very fact that Paul has to argue, in light of enemy-love, that the people should forsake (violent) resistance reveals that the "governing authorities" are, in some sense, worthy of revolt. Much like Jesus' call to turn the other cheek, this passage recognizes that, under normal circumstances, one would hit back. To refrain from violence is a testimony to the Roman Christians' goodness, not the goodness of Rome.

The admonition to "be subject" is offered because "the authorities that exist have been established by God." This word translated as "established" (or in other translations as "ordained" or "instituted") would seem to argue for a divine ordinance of governmental authority. However, John Howard Yoder has (rightly) challenged translating the Greek word *tetagmenai* (from the verb *tassō*) in any of these ways. Rather, Yoder argues that a better translation would be that the authorities are ordered or "put in line" by God. Therefore, Paul could be advising his readers against revolt since God is already dealing with the rulers.[20]

It is also important to note the way in which a substantial cultural gap plays into any treatment of this passage. The word translated in this passage as "authorities" or "authority" is *exousia*. Due to the nature of translation and the dualism in our modern imaginations (separating spiritual from political realms), we don't often recognize that Paul's use of the word *exousia* blurs the distinction between political and spiritual realities. See some of the ways the word is translated in other passages attributed to Paul:

- 1 Corinthians 15:24: Then the end will come, when he hands
  over the kingdom to God the Father after he has destroyed all
  dominion, *authority* and power.

- Ephesians 1:19-21: That power is the same as the mighty strength
  he exerted when he raised Christ from the dead and seated him
  at his right hand in the heavenly realms, far above all rule and
  authority, power and dominion, and every name that is invoked,
  not only in the present age but also in the one to come.

- Ephesians 6:12: For our struggle is not against flesh and blood,
  but against the rulers, against the *authorities*, against the powers
  of this dark world and against the spiritual forces of evil in the
  heavenly realms.

- Colossians 2:15: And having disarmed the powers and *authorities*, he made a public spectacle of them, triumphing over them
  by the cross.

When he uses words like *authorities* or *rulers* or *powers*, Paul
may be talking primarily about spiritual realities, political realities
or perhaps both at the same time. This adds complexity to what
would otherwise seem like a straightforward challenge to be
"subject" to the "authorities" because, elsewhere, such "authorities"
are seen as enemies to Christ.

Finally, it is a mistake to take Romans 13 as a universal message
of how Christians everywhere ought to relate to government. Wes
Howard-Brook states:

> We can say, though, that whatever Paul meant to convey to
> the Christians at Rome in the 50s, it was not a general prin-
> ciple of subservience to imperial authority . . . we've seen
> how Paul's letters regularly insist on attributing to Jesus titles
> and authority that his audience would certainly have heard
> as "plagiarized" from Roman sources. . . . The most likely

explanation of Romans 13 is that it was a message addressed to specific concerns of Roman Christians under Nero.[21]

And so, from Paul's perspective, the Christians in Rome in the 50s should not revolt. Rather, they should love their oppressors and leave wrath to God. This wasn't because the Roman government was good but because followers of Jesus are called to the way of love. Furthermore, God has put the authorities in line and will judge them.

Much could be said about what Romans 13 could mean for us. At the very least, it encourages us to trust God and love our enemies. While Paul argues against violent resistance, his words leave room for nonviolent struggle. It would be foolish, I think, to extrapolate universal principles of governmental engagement from this passage. Nevertheless, once we understand Paul's sentiments, we can better discern how to express the love of God in our own contexts.

What about "render unto Caesar"? Tied for the most referenced antianarchy passage is Mark 12:13-17:

> Later they sent some of the Pharisees and Herodians to Jesus to catch him in his words. They came to him and said, "Teacher, we know that you are a man of integrity. You aren't swayed by others, because you pay no attention to who they are; but you teach the way of God in accordance with the truth. Is it right to pay the imperial tax to Caesar or not? Should we pay or shouldn't we?"
>
> But Jesus knew their hypocrisy. "Why are you trying to trap me?" he asked. "Bring me a denarius and let me look at it." They brought the coin, and he asked them, "Whose image is this? And whose inscription?"
>
> "Caesar's," they replied.
>
> Then Jesus said to them, "Give back to Caesar what is Caesar's and to God what is God's."
>
> And they were amazed at him.

Clearly they were trying to trick Jesus into publicly picking sides—and either would be dangerous. If he sided with Rome, he'd lose the support of the people. If he denounced Rome, he'd be a marked man. The fact that Herodians and Pharisees are working together against Jesus is noteworthy; Jesus was enough of a threat to cause two rival factions to join forces.

Are the implications that we should create a distinction between church and state? Or even split them into two separate kingdoms with different claims, as Luther or some Anabaptists have advocated? No. This is a very smart slap against Caesar without simply denouncing Caesar. By pointing to their coin (no good Jew should have a graven image like a coin in their pocket to begin with), Jesus is exposing idolatry and saying that such things already belong to Caesar, not God. If you've got any Caesar-stuff, it should be rendered accordingly. But what is God's belongs to God. Or, as Dorothy Day is reputed to have said, "If we rendered unto God all the things that belong to God, there would be nothing left for Caesar."

Lest you think that such approaches to Scripture are a recent innovation, I direct you to Irenaeus. Irenaeus was a second-century bishop on the fringes of the empire in Lugdunum, Gaul. He was a disciple of Polycarp, who was a disciple of the apostle John. In other words, he was removed from Jesus by two generations; he was a friend of a friend of Jesus:

> The Lord himself directed us to "render unto Caesar the things which are Caesar's, and to God the things which are God's," naming Caesar as Caesar, but confessing God as God. In like manner also, that which says, "You cannot serve two masters," he does himself interpret, saying "You cannot serve God and mammon," acknowledging God as God but mentioning mammon, a thing also having an existence. He does not call mammon Lord when he says, "You cannot serve two

masters," but he teaches his disciples who serve God not to be subject to mammon nor to be ruled by it.[22]

In other words, Irenaeus believed that the thing we should render Caesar is our renunciation. Caesar's lordship is comparable to that of mammon.[23] He is only your lord if you are his slave.

◆　◆　◆

My hope in offering this quick overview of the Scriptures is not to satisfy every troubling question. Rather, I've shown the rough contours of a lens: a lens that forswears empire and, instead, opts for liberation for all people. My intention is not to offer a novel reading of Scripture but to draw attention to themes that have been there all along, buried under centuries of theological justification.

The remainder of this book is my attempt at answering: "So now what?"

ABBA PRAYER

Subvert this society of spiritual insincerity!
These pseudo-saints wear masks of metaphysical maturity
veiling their vulgar visage and voluminous villainy
Prattling proudly, they publicly proclaim their piety. It's pathetic!
Don't buy it, brother. Don't get snared, sister.
As for you, Do the prayers you do . . .
In the quiet place. Simple words. Unclenched.
Like little kids, call for papa and cry for your heaven-momma.
Yes, Abba shaped the universe in secret,
but still closer to you than you are to yourself.
Release your held breath and pray:
We need a regime change!
Not Obama, O, abba-momma.
We need liberation,
From this Bush generation
The violence must stop, O, abba-pop.
An end to this administration
To a divine nation.
A Divinization.
We don't need laptops and lattes,
Macbooks or machiattos.
We don't need Ronald McDonald
Or Little Debbie
Famous Dave or Colonel Sanders.
The Red Baron, Jack-in-the-Box, and
The Burger King living in their White Castle.
With subjects fat and starved . . .
We dull eyed slaves . . .
consume our liberties.

All we need is what we need . . .

Bread . . .

right now.

You.

We beg

For debt forgiveness.

Our bedrooms are wallpapered with past-due notices

Homes built upon a mountain of bones.

Cars in our three-stall garages run off the fumes of oppression.

Our lawns fertilized with speeches of leaders.

So we declare bankruptcy!

As the sheriff bars windows and doors.

And we step out over the broken picket fence

To join the protestors occupying the street.

Decrying destitution! Denouncing debt!

Dreaming of democracy.

But, when opportunity arises,

When we too arise to power

And cross back over that fence to take back houses with new mortgages

And lawns

with pesticide purified pristinity

in grids of cement

Cracked people.

Happified by dancing pixels.

Abba.

Deliver us! From delicious diversions that dirty our divinity!

Deliver us! From discontented devouring.

Deliver us, to delight.

To love. Together. To see spirit, swimming in our shared space.

Singing a new song of sensuality.

Abba. Between us.

Abba. In us.

Abba. Above us.

Abba. Beneath us.

Abba. Here.

Abba. Now.

Abba.

Abba.

Abba.

Amen.

Seven

Encountering the Feral God

Jesus is dead in the buildings
and in the cities and in the outside.
But he is alive in our hearts.

St. Jonas of Minneapolis

Ours is a civilized god. He is distant, floating high above the world, refusing to be dirtied by it. He is the supreme hierarch, the ruler of all. The great architect, looking down over all of creation and ordering it according to his divine blueprint. Of all of the things he's created, he likes human beings the best. Sometimes he communicates to some of these humans, revealing to them part of his divine blueprint. Our primary relationship with this god is one of obedience; we are to do his will so that things can work according to the blueprint.

This god works well with imperialism. Imperialism is about ordering creation. It is about obedience. It is about mastery. This god is the creation of an imperial imagination.

The god we have shaped in our image has re-created humanity. We too live above the world, separate from it. As abstracted from it as our god is from us. We live in a world of distances—where humanity is separated from God, where person is alienated from person and where we have forsaken our creatureliness to rule creation. Ours is a lonely world.

In order to make sense of our chaotic, lonely world, we create blueprints of our own and try to control what is around us to conform it to that blueprint. We do this because we worship a blueprinting god. Insofar as we worship this god-with-a-blueprint whose first requirement is obedience (understood in its traditional, monological sense), we place ourselves in a story of imperialism.

Some may balk at this. Many Christians, after all, have found a way to worship a god who demands obedience and, at the same time, live in ways of mutuality, love and humility in their own lives. Nevertheless, I suspect there is an unresolved tension within their minds and hearts: Why does this god act in one way and then call me to another? In the end, they accept some sort of divine exceptionalism. Much like the United States (or any other empire) holds itself to a different standard than subordinate nations, so too this god can commit acts of genocide, violence and oppression while (without any sense of irony) telling us to love our enemies, turn the other cheek and practice mutual submission. It is one step from worshiping such an exceptional god to embracing imperialism in his name.

Before I go further, I want to clarify a bit what I'm getting at when I say *obedience*. I'm not encouraging divine disobedience (not exactly). Rather, I'm advocating for a reimagining of what obedience looks like. And a reimagining of our image of God. I believe God's concern is primarily for us to be like Jesus, not simply to act like Jesus through obedience.

John 15 (where Jesus says, "I no longer call you servants") seems to point in a direction that challenges conventional notions of obedience. It is interesting that Jesus says, in the same breath, "I no longer call you servants" and "you are my friends if you do what I command" (John 15:15, 14). This seems kind of strange, until you examine the nature of the command: to love. Here Jesus is offering an understanding of obedience that is different. It is no longer monological (I say and you do) but dialogical (we are now friends). Just as the lordship of Jesus subverts our notions of reign, so too does Jesus' call to obedience subvert our notions of obedience.

When you have a lord who undoes lordship and a master who subverts mastery, then everything is different. I think it is a mistake to assume that obedience to such a one is at all similar to other patterns of obedience.

This line of thought is hardly original. I first encountered such unsettling (and liberating) thoughts in the writings of Dorothee Sölle, who writes:

> Can one demand a particular stance toward God and educate toward that stance, yet simultaneously criticize that same stance toward people and toward institutions? Is it actually possible, in the realities of daily life, to distinguish between the obedience which is due God and that obedience toward people which we can and ought with good reason refuse? I suspect that we Christians today have the duty to criticize the entire concept of obedience, and that this criticism must be radical, simply because we do not know exactly who God is and what God, at any given moment, wills. It is no longer possible to describe our relationship to God with a formal concept that is limited to the mere performance of duties. We cannot remove ourselves from history if we wish to speak seriously about God. And in our Christian history, our history of the 20th century, obedience has played a catastrophic role.[1]

Sölle isn't suggesting the abandonment of obedience, as though we should rebel against God. Rather, she suggests a reexamination of obedience in light of Jesus' witness:

[Obedience] does not mean the carrying out of commands, and most assuredly not in the sense of Benedict's continually repeated decision to obey the abbot the way Christ obeyed God. Obedience means instead a decision which first discovers God's will in doing. The person herself must decide what is to be done; she is not the fulfiller of assigned commands. Nothing is here taken from the autonomy of the subject. The will of God does not present external demands and it is not predetermined or fixed . . . It is not God in a general, timeless sense who demands obedience, but the situation which demands a response, and only therein does God require a person's response . . . an obedience which has its eyes wide open, which first discovers God's will in the situation, a discerning obedience.[2]

Our relationship with God shapes our relationship to one another and to the land. If that relationship is seen primarily as that of subjects to the supreme hierarch, our imaginations will tend toward imperialism.

Let me be practical. Even the most basic act—offering food to a stranger—can be radically different depending upon how it is held in our imaginations. Offering bread can be a condescending act of charity to those "less fortunate" or a step toward justice as bread is shared among equals around the table of Jesus. From the outside, the act of offering food to a stranger may look the same, but its liberating potential is often determined by our hearts, and our hearts are often shaped by what we love the most. Jesus said, "Where your treasure is, there your heart will be also" (Matthew 6:21). The god we worship matters.

In the Hebrew Scriptures, whenever the people had been se-
duced by imperial images of God, the voices of the prophets would
echo calls of repentance from the margins. As Wes Howard-Brook
suggests, the prophetic voice calls us out of the religion of empire
to embrace the religion[3] of creation:

> We can understand one of the Bible's religions to be
> grounded in the *experience of and ongoing relationship with
> the Creator God*, leading to a covenantal bond between that
> God and God's people for the blessing and abundance of *all*
> people and *all* creation. The other, while sometimes
> *claiming* to be grounded in that same God, is actually a
> human invention used to justify and legitimate attitudes
> and behaviors that provide blessing and abundance for
> *some* at *the expense of others*.[4]

The prophets call us to worship the God who is the source of life,
the giver of life. This God is a creative, feral spring from which our
own lives pour. We encounter this God in the wild places, where
life is unfettered. We encounter this God when we name and let go
(repent) of those structures that trammel life and subjugate people
and the land.

Ours is a world in need of prophets and mystics. The Hebrew
prophets spoke from the wilderness, a place without cities and
kings and temples. The wilderness is a place of creation—where a
person is free to be a creature. It is a place where pretenses are
stripped away, where the distances can collapse.

They remind us that faith is not a tool of domination. Faith is a
feral force that sets us free to love and encounter each other
without a blueprint.

Howard-Brook writes: "Moses encountered YHWH outside of
Egypt, outside of empire, in the *wilderness* and at a *mountain*. These
two sites are the repeated places in which YHWH encounters

Israel."[5] Moses meets God in a place free from civilization, apart from the city. Apart from the place of domination.

It is significant that before Jesus begins his ministry, he goes into the wild:

> At once the Spirit sent him out into the wilderness, and he was in the wilderness forty days, being tempted by Satan. He was with the wild animals, and angels attended him. (Mark 1:12-13)

Notice that even though Jesus is "alone," he is not alone. The distance has collapsed. The Spirit has brought him to the wild place, where he is in fellowship with creation (with the wild animals), and even the veil of heaven is opened as he fellowships with the angels. Even Satan is present, to be confronted for what he is.

The wilderness is the place of unvarnished truth. I'm not suggesting that if we merely go into the woods, all truth will be revealed. Nor am I suggesting that being in a city necessarily taints us. Nevertheless, it is in the wilderness—the place of creatureliness—that Jesus encounters the world as it is. And he brings that feral faith with him all the way to the temple, where he confronts the religion of empire.

The religion of empire is presented by Satan—to use economic, political and religious power to enforce the messianic agenda. But Jesus said no to three temptations and, angry at the devil, chose a different way. The wilderness was the place where Jesus spoke the truth to Satan (the animating force of empire) and became, himself, the path to liberation.

We need to rewild our faith, to reject our assumptions about religion and power and sustenance. Our most pressing need is for practices that help us see the world through a different lens than that of imperial myths and civilizational programming.

The feral faith of Jesus probably has more in common with

traditional tribal spirituality than it does with what we think of as "Christianity." In the prophetic tradition, and in the experience of Jesus, the feral God is found primarily in creation, not in a temple. This isn't to say that God is absent in holy buildings. But it is perhaps fair to say that God is present to us more in spite of our holy accoutrements and machinations rather than because of them.

PRACTICES FOR ENCOUNTERING THE FERAL GOD

So, what does this rewilding look like? I want to be careful not to offer a list of things to fix our faith, as though offering a blueprint can fix our addiction to blueprints. However, I have found three practices to be useful in helping me encounter the feral God. They aren't magical practices. But they can provide a way for us to encounter the feral God.

Practice one: experimenting with God. It is tragic that the way of Jesus has become a disembodied set of principles. We need to relearn the way of Jesus—not simply by rereading Scripture, but by relearning how to see Scripture. Our challenge isn't in finding the right content but in reading things with the right eyes. How we learn is perhaps more important than what we learn. Most of us, I suspect, have learned quite a bit about Jesus but haven't been encouraged by our churches to learn from Jesus or to learn in the way Jesus taught. Because of this, we've treated our discipleship like a math class: crack open a book, learn the content and hope (somehow) it will make (someday) a difference in our lives.

This approach is so entrenched that any attempt to practice the way of Jesus is seen as extreme. And, depending upon our political orientation, this extremity is either praised or ridiculed.

In 2003, my wife and I formed Missio Dei (which is now called the Mennonite Worker) with a simple premise: we would simply read the Gospels and ask three questions as we read:

1. What is Jesus saying or doing in this passage?

2. What excuses are stirring in our minds as a way of justifying why we shouldn't do likewise?

3. What is at least one thing we can do to walk in the direction of what Jesus is saying or doing?

These questions eventually led us into becoming an intentional community that centered its life around the practice of hospitality. The approach was largely experimental; there were no preset notions of what it should look like to follow the way of Jesus. Nor were we trying to push ourselves to new heights of heroism. Rather, we challenged one another to be honest with our fears and recognize at least one step we could take.

My own spirit of experimentation deepened in coming years as I became friends with Mark Scandrette. His community in San Francisco had been engaging in an innovative (yet ancient) approach to learning the way of Jesus that Mark dubbed the "Jesus Dojo." The idea wasn't simply to experiment more deeply into the way of Jesus, but to treat this experimentation as a way of learning.

One experiment they did involved living into John the Baptist's command in Luke 3:11 that anyone who has two tunics should share with the one who has none. As a result, Mark and his friends decided to sell half of their possessions and give the money to the poor. This act wasn't treated as an end in itself. Rather, throughout the process they discussed with one another the thoughts and feelings that surfaced. The idea wasn't simply to help the poor but also to examine their own hearts and transform their relationship with material goods. Instead of assuming they had done a good deed by putting the teachings of Jesus into practice, they approached their divestment as a way of learning the way of Jesus.

The goal of an experimental faith isn't to "get things right." Such a way of seeing the world is static and lifeless. Rather, truth is dynamic and relational. It allows us to learn new things about ourselves and our God. It opens us to encounter the feral God in our midst who shows us a new way. The goal isn't to obey abstract rules but to enter into a relationship with Jesus, to learn from Jesus, to become more like Jesus.

Practice two: embracing our creatureliness. If we want to encounter a wild God, we need to embrace our creatureliness. Just as Jesus linked love of God with love of neighbor, I believe we must link love of neighbor with a love of creation. They are all linked. War emerges out of our greed for "natural resources" and our lust for land exploitation. Violence and dehumanization are almost always linked to a broken relationship with creation. This runs counter to modern propaganda, which sees previous generations as increasingly violent. We have a false assumption that civilization brings peacefulness.

To rewild our faith requires reacquainting ourselves with creation. And one of the most practical ways to reorient ourselves with creation is to change our relationship with food. There are a number of ways of experimenting with one's relationship with food—from fasting to gardening to fishing. The goal here is to enter into an experiment wherein we engage food in a different way, a way that helps us to see ourselves as a part of creation rather than as beings who live above creation.

One simple practice that has helped me deepen my relationship with the rest of creation is the simple act of cooking a meal. To me, cooking a meal is like making a sand mandala. In Hinduism and Buddhism, a mandala is a geometric pattern that represents the universe. Buddhist monks have a practice where they create beautiful mandalas out of colored sand. When the mandala is finished, they sweep it clean and start anew. The practice of making sand mandalas is an exercise in impermanence. Like life, it is fleeting and dynamic.

Likewise, making a wonderful meal for friends, family or strangers is an exercise in impermanence. Days before, the food that has now found its way onto a plate was still in the soil. Ideally in soil nearby. It was grown in a garden or in a field and was picked and prepared with love into a complex collection of flavors, colors, textures and smells. Every plate is a work of art that still contains life, which we consume so that we may live.

When I cook, I don't think about what happened earlier in the day. Nor do I worry about what will happen later in the day. I think about the food. To me, cooking should be done attentively, focusing simply on the act of creating the meal itself.

And when it is ready, I bring it to friends, who are waiting at the table. Some of those friends may have grown the food. Or they rescued it from a dumpster. Or maybe one of them bought it at a local market. The whole process, from the soil to the kitchen to the plate to the stomach, is itself the art form. And in its impermanence it is a form of worship.

It is a form of worship that some of us practice several times a day. It is so mundane we can take it for granted. But when we do it attentively and reflect upon the story of the food, we find ourselves participating in creation. A simple meal. What one person sees as a distraction that keeps them from more important things, another person may call "Eucharist." And Eucharist is one of those practices that holds the potential to heal rifts that exist between me and someone who I have hurt, between me and my God, and between me and creation.

Eucharist can be practiced as a sort of ritual with a bit of wine and bread. However, every meal can be Eucharistic. How we gather around the table can help heal our relationship with the land when the food we eat is sustainable and honors the fragility of the earth. The time around the table can heal my relationships with the people in my life if the table becomes a place of acceptance, equality and attention that I carry with me beyond dinner. And the table can serve to bring healing to my relationship with God if I listen to the voice of the Spirit in the voices of those gathered and remember that my brother Jesus once ate a meal with his friends before his crucifixion.

Practice three: silence. Most of our lives are loud. It seems to me that most of humanity throughout most of history has experienced ample amounts of silence. Silence was once abundant. Now I find it scarce. Machines hum, music blares, people shout. Rarely do I experience silence. Though, to be honest, rarely do I welcome it. Silence can be violent—forcing me to sit with myself and my own screaming thoughts.

But silence has become a way for me to let go of the false images of God in my head. In silence, where I am free from distraction, I can pray the prayer of Meister Eckhart: "God, rid me of God." As various anxieties and random notions enter my mind, I gently dismiss them until I am at peace. And then, like Elijah in the cave at Mount Horeb, the voice of God sometimes comes to me in a gentle whisper.

I used to assume that when God spoke, it was to give me instructions or unveil new truths. But I find that whenever I dismiss everything that isn't of God (as Simone Weil suggests), whatever remains is God. And as I rest in God's presence, I try to resist the temptation to expect anything of God. Rather, I sit. As I sit in silence with God, I trust that God is at work within my soul in unseen, wild ways.

◆ ◆ ◆

Of course, these practices are merely a beginning. We are creative beings. I will find new practices that help me let go of the civilized god in my mind. Each of us have our own journey. If these practices help you, then practice them, but move deeper. The challenge is to keep experimenting. Some practices will become like trusted friends. But there is always room for new friends. May we all remain open to the wild voice of God, a voice that threatens to tear down the walls that keep us safely in our cages.

Eight

Walking with the
Compassionate Christ

Attention is the rarest and purest
form of generosity.

SIMONE WEIL

Jesus' ministry was wonderfully gritty. It wasn't abstract.
Jesus made good on his Luke 4 platform by actually proclaiming
good news to the poor, setting people free from social exclusion,
healing the sick, casting out demons, giving sight to the blind.
Sure, there were spiritual implications, but Jesus didn't spiritualize his message. The acts of tangible healing didn't point to a
deeper truth. They were, in themselves, a work of liberation and
spirituality. He began on the ground, with the people, in a remarkably nonabstract, tangible way.

Yet we start in the opposite way. Often, we spiritualize Jesus and
his message and treat the tangible stuff as a sort of heroic option.
Some abstract the gospel by spiritualizing it, to the point that the
gospel becomes nothing but fodder for books and sermons.

Others abstract the gospel by programming it, to the point where people check the gospel off their list by voting, doing charity work or simply donating their money to professionals who do the work on the charity on their behalf. Charity, in either case, accepts the unjust arrangement. As Paulo Freire suggests: "The generosity of the oppressors is nourished by an unjust order, which must be maintained in order to justify that generosity . . . The man or woman who proclaims devotion to the cause of liberation yet is unable to enter into *communion* with the people, whom he or she continues to regard as totally ignorant, is grievously self-deceived."[1]

Both of these general approaches increase the distance between us and suffering. We become apathetic to the struggles and sufferings around us. Apathy comes from a Greek word *apatheia*, which is made up of two words: *a* meaning "without" and *pathos* meaning "suffering." Of this, Dorothee Sölle writes:

> Apathy is a form of the inability to suffer. It is understood as a social condition in which people are so dominated by the goal of avoiding suffering that it becomes a goal to avoid human relationships and contacts altogether. In so far as the experiences of suffering, the *pathai* [Greek for the things that happen to a person, misfortunes] of life are repressed, there is a corresponding disappearance of passion for life and of the strength and intensity of its joys. Without question this ideal bears the imprint of middle-class consciousness.[2]

Jesus rejects apathy. Instead, his is a way of compassion. Compassion comes from the Latin word that means "to suffer with." Compassion rejects apathy and alienation and bridges the distance between persons. Compassion is easily understood, in our society, as a sentiment. Perhaps this is because our society has so thoroughly inherited the separation of action from intention that we feel sentiment is all that is required to be a loving human being. But in Jesus there is no separation between intention and action. His action reflects his heart, just as his life reflects the very life of God.

Rather than a weak sentiment, or a condescending act of charity, compassion is prophetic. Those with compassion refuse to accept the world as it is and enter into injustice and brokenness. Compassion is the practice of mysticism, because it collapses the distances between us. And, in bridging the distance, compassion exposes the principalities and powers and myths that breed alienation and separation.

In his classic work, *The Prophetic Imagination*, Walter Brueggemann puts it this way:

> Compassion constitutes a radical form of criticism, for it announces that the hurt is to be taken seriously, that the hurt is not to be accepted as normal and natural but is an abnormal and unacceptable condition for humanness. . . . Thus the compassion of Jesus is to be understood not simply as a personal emotional reaction but as a public criticism in which he dares to act upon his concern against the entire numbness of his social context. Empires live by numbness. Empires, in their militarism, expect numbness about the human cost of war. Corporate economies expect blindness to the cost in terms of poverty and exploitation. Governments and societies of domination go to great lengths to keep the numbness intact. Jesus penetrates the numbness by his compassion and with his compassion takes the first step by making visible the odd abnormality that had become business as usual. Thus compassion that might be seen simply as generous goodwill is in fact criticism of the system, forces, and ideologies that produce the hurt. Jesus enters into the hurt and finally comes to embody it.[3]

The way of Jesus is the way of compassion. It involves sharing life with those around us and suffering with them. I want to be careful here; embracing the suffering of others doesn't require that we treat suffering like a holy fetish. There is a danger in this, particularly for Christians. We worship the One who suffered on a cross. But, as Dorothee Sölle writes, the cross is not

> a symbol of masochism which needs suffering in order to convince itself of love. It is above all a symbol of reality. Love does not "require" the cross, but *de facto* it ends up on the cross. *De facto* Jesus of Nazareth was crucified. . . . Love does not cause suffering or produce it, though it must necessarily seek confrontation, since its most important concern is not the avoidance of suffering but the liberation of people.[4]

Jesus went to the cross as an act of solidarity with the oppressed. The cross is God confronting the world with compassion.

◆   ◆   ◆

As I shared in the introduction, my first mystical experience happened when I was fourteen. As I sat with other teens around a campfire, I experienced the suffering of the world. In the twenty-or-so years since I've reflected back upon that experience, I've become convinced that it was an invitation to compassion. Throughout my life, I've struggled to accept that invitation.

Every day, when I wake up, I'm aware of my own feelings of alienation. I feel disconnected from people. I feel distant from their pain—even the people I live with—and my own desire to show love and compassion doesn't flow easily. I'm one of those people who loves hugs but is afraid to initiate them.[5]

I tell you this because I don't want you to assume that showing compassion comes easily for me. My own attempts at trying to collapse the distance between me and other human beings has been awkward.

I'll give you a quick example. When folks cry around me (which happens from time to time), I kind of just sit there, looking awkwardly at them. I sometimes ask myself, "What would a compassionate person do in this situation?" My assumption is that, when a friend or acquaintance cries, a compassionate person would reach out and hug them or put a hand on their shoulder or something that signifies human connection.

But what I do in such situations is panic inside. I start saying to myself, "Crap, crap, crap, what do I do?" Usually, in the end, what happens is I offer to go make them something to eat. When all else fails, I fall back on what I know.

Yet, as flawed of a "wounded healer" as I am, I know I'm more compassionate now than I was last year. And a year ago, I was more compassionate than I was the year before. I am growing in compassion.

One of the temptations I've struggled to overcome is to equate compassion with charity. I've alluded to this earlier but would like to explore it in further depth here.

Often, First-World Christians respond to injustice with charity. Charity never challenges structures of oppression. In fact, charity allows the wealthy and powerful to stay in their position of domination while feeling justified. After all, they are generous with their "earned" wealth. Meanwhile the dispossessed, poor and marginalized are kept in their place. So much of what begins as a pursuit for justice becomes mere charity in the end.

Charity doesn't, by itself, challenge social relationships. It accepts things as they are and attempts to share a modest amount of abundance from the "fortunate" with the "less fortunate," or the "blessed" with the "needy." What happens when our institutions bring charity and imperial attitudes into the margins? The history of Christianity shows that the recipients of our "help" become imperial converts who internalize oppression—often assuming that their poverty is their own fault and that, if they are going to be liberated, they need to become like those who give them charity. We can, unintentionally, make imperial converts.

If we attempt to bring about social justice and relational transformation without first taking a posture of *Gelassenheit*, we will presumptuously carry our imperialism with us into the margins. We must yield our hearts to God for decolonization. Out of love of God and neighbor, I need to name the habits, attitudes and privileges that are mine by virtue of being an educated, white American male, and submit them to God.

Before we can see the kingdom reality, we must first repent of the old order. Before we can experience the joy of the unkingdom, we must mourn over the empire. The way of the true radical—the way of the prophet—is to open our eyes to the alternative reality that is the unkingdom and to grieve and mourn over the world to which we still cling. Sure, there is still room for anger. But above that rises repentance and lament.

We must mourn the old world, the old ways and its cycle of death—the cycle of greed and violence and oppression—as we move into the unkingdom of God. And, as we do so, we must let go of the illusion of our own righteousness. We can't render ourselves radicals because we happen to have superficially opted out of the system and picked up a new vocabulary.

If we are able to live the part of the radical without mourning our own complicity and mourning for those trapped in the cycle, we are simply a clanging cymbal. If, because of some strong exercise of willpower, we manage to—based upon the heat of our own frustration—carve out an entire way of life that stands in contrast to the empire, but have not love, we are simply the beat of an angry drum.

Too often justice work has the goal of turning marginalized folks into middle-class Americans. Perhaps our affluence is a deeper problem than their poverty.

Contemporary Christianity is filled with folks who believe themselves to be in "solidarity" with all sorts of oppressed people but somehow haven't really changed their way of life or the nature of their social lives. We can't challenge injustice by donating money or reading a book. We can't combat racism simply by going to a conference. We don't confront sexism by simply changing the pronouns in our writing and speaking. All of these things are perhaps essential steps in the journey. But they aren't the destination. More needs to change than sentiment. We need to move from charity to compassion. Charity is the sharing of resources. Compassion is the sharing of life and the suffering we experience in life.

PRACTICES FOR WALKING WITH THE COMPASSIONATE CHRIST

So how can we deepen our capacity for compassion? Do we simply muster up the will to do good deeds? Do we read inspirational tales of the saints? Again, I am not going to tell you to do things like practice hospitality or start a soup kitchen. Those may be compassionate acts, but they may also be condescending. Rather, I offer the following practices as things that have helped me deepen in compassion for those around me.

Practice one: localizing our imaginations. We need to tell the stories of the places in which we live from the vantage point of the oppressed. If we are going to develop practices that show love to one another and the land under our feet, we need to embrace the confessional practice of truth-telling. When I remember that my city, Minneapolis, was born as a staging area to force the Dakota out of land that was deemed more suitable for white settlers, the imperial myths that stifle my imagination lose some of their power over me.

Furthermore, we need to honestly tell the story of how we relate to the places in which we live. If I am going to come to terms with the domination in my own heart, I need to explore my identity in relationship to the place in which I live. This is the only way I can begin to break the "spell" over my imagination that sees myself as an American citizen, or as an individual consumer, or as a thing called a "white man."

One way I practice this happens whenever I take my son to Minnehaha Park in South Minneapolis. Minnehaha Park is near Fort Snelling. Though it is a sacred place to the Dakota, the only monuments there celebrate the European settling of this land. When I take Jonas there, I call it "Oppressor Park" and tell him the story of how white people came to this land. I tell him that the state of Minnesota took the land from the Dakota to make space for white settlers. I also tell him where our family came from (various places in Western Europe) and that while our family didn't take the land, we too are settlers.

I tell him this and then ask him what he thinks about it. Usually, Jonas says something like, "Minnesota should give Oppressor Park back to the Dakota people." I want him to grow up understanding that he is a settler so that he too can escape the allure of imperial myths and, instead, embrace the unkingdom. In a very important way, telling my little boy such things is my own act of repentance. We tend to tell children (consciously or not) what we hold most true and valuable. By telling him the story of the land, I give myself the freedom to choose a different way. I can either be a happy imperial citizen, or I can work through the layers of conditioning and myth and propaganda and begin, slowly, to relate to the world in truth.

Practice two: paying attention to what is happening in front of us. Speaking of brainwashing my son, I try to take him to protests from time to time. My son Jonas committed his first act of civil disobedience when he was a little over a year old. He and I were both guilty of trespassing, but a passerby would have seen a father and son playing in a backyard of a typical South Minneapolis home. As Jonas and I played in the yard with some friends from our faith community, a handful of activists and concerned neighbors were gathered inside lending their support to Rosemary Williams, a woman who had owned the property for over twenty years and lived on the block for fifty-five years. Like millions of other US-Americans, Rosemary was facing foreclosure. We were there to hold off the coming eviction, which happened several months later. Over the past few years, I've taken my son to a handful of protests. He's witnessed an FBI raid, stood with me in solidarity with exploited workers and undocumented friends, and challenged war. I don't assume our attendance at protests does the world any good—at least not directly. I don't protest to effect change in the world. I protest to effect change in me and to show my son a different image of the world.

On September 24, 2010, FBI agents raided six homes in Minneapolis (and two in Chicago) looking for links to "terrorist activity." The eight respected peace activists who were raided had recently traveled to Colombia and the Palestinian territories. Such travel is perfectly legal, but because the eight people regularly protested against US military involvement in those regions, they were flagged.

Jonas was almost three when we went to the FBI raid. That sounds scarier than it is. I loaded him into his bicycle trailer and rode up to Hard Times Cafe off of Riverside Avenue in Minneapolis. The raid was happening at the apartment above the cafe. The agents were dressed casually as they came out of the apartment door with boxes of confiscated documents and hard drives. Meanwhile, the subject of the raid—a local union organizer and peace activist—was downstairs sitting at the cafe, talking to a local reporter.

I told Jonas what was happening as best as I could. That these guys called the FBI were taking the stuff of a man who only wanted people to stop hurting each other.

When we entered the cafe, I walked over to the activist. Jonas had a concerned look on his face. He said to the man, "I'm sad that those mean FBI guys took your things!" He responded naturally, with compassion. He saw someone experiencing injustice and extended concern.

The next day, we went to a protest outside of the FBI building. A number of peace activists had been raided that day, and the peace community was upset. I wanted Jonas to be ready for the protest, so I went to the local thrift store and bought him a proper uniform—a black turtleneck with an army-green blazer. I thought looking like a beatnik would help him look the part of a protestor.

The presence of a little beatnik protestor at the rally added a human factor, I think. Jonas slowly picked up the chants of the protestors. He heard them chanting, "Stand up, fight back!" He too began the chant. When things quieted down for someone to speak, he screamed, "Stand up, fight back!" as loudly as he could. A few dozen people began to chuckle, including the two agents standing at the front door, observing the situation.

This is, of course, not a daily occurrence. Usually, walking in compassion with others involves sitting with guests in our home or acquaintances we meet on the street. Wherever humanity is, there is an opportunity for compassion. Compassion begins with paying attention. Simone Weil once said that attention is the rarest and purest form of generosity.

It is easy to be overwhelmed with news reports of violent crime and wars and drought and poverty. In fact, it is almost impossible to be anything

My son Jonas, protesting wunderkind.

but apathetic about such things, since they are so abstract and huge. This is why, when I read a news report about hundreds dying in a natural disaster or of over a hundred thousand civilian deaths in Iraq it doesn't hit me nearly as hard as hearing about a little four-year-old girl getting shot in my city, or receiving the news that my grandmother has passed away. Logic doesn't dictate our response to suffering; our proximity to suffering dictates our response to suffering. If we want to challenge the injustices of the world, we need to pay attention to them as they happen around us and respond to them.

Practice three: learning in the margins. Humans are not able to find true compassion, nor create structures of deep transformation, without entering into Jesus' own compassion, which is incarnate in the poor and marginalized. Being "aware" of social injustice doesn't collapse the alienation experienced between human beings. We must nurture real relationships, relatively free from agenda, before we develop strong conclusions around what justice looks like.

There is a temptation to assume that those in the margins are more "needy" than you. Or that they are "less fortunate." Yet Jesus said: "Blessed are the poor." One could fathom the depth of that insight for a lifetime. At the very least, however, it might suggest that the affluent have more to learn at the feet of the poor than they have to teach. I'd like to suggest that we strike such condescending language regarding the poor, the marginalized or the ostracized. Rather, in a nonsentimentalizing way, let us see our fellow human beings with open eyes, to see the world they inhabit for what it is and see the world with them.

As we break bread in the margins, and the alienation narrows, we may begin to suffer with our new friends. Not a heroic suffering—when we suffer with the oppressed, it isn't a heroic suffering on behalf of another. Rather, we are experiencing a suffering that is ours as well, one that our apathy and privilege has walled away from us.

Lila Watson wrote: "If you have come here to help me, then you are wasting your time. . . . But if you have come because your liberation is bound up with mine, then let us work together."[6] By embracing a life of compassion—by suffering with others—we discover our own deep humanity and can begin to live life without abstraction. It is with the marginalized we can experience the unkingdom of God.

◆   ◆   ◆

Compassion is costly, but without it, suffering remains. We cannot ignore suffering if we want to see its end. We cannot turn our back on oppression and injustice, nor can we legislate it away. The way of Jesus calls us to compassion. And compassion is something we experience as we learn from Christ in the margins, for that is where Christ dwells. In the words of sixteenth-century Anabaptist martyr Anna of Rotterdam, "Where you hear of the Cross, there is Christ."[7]

Let us go to the places of suffering and learn the way of Jesus.

Nine

Discerning the Subversive Spirit

*They paint the Holy Spirit descending upon the Apostles' heads
in the form of a dove. For shame! Haven't they ever felt the
Holy Spirit burning them? Where did they find that innocent,
edible bird? How can they present that to us as Spirit? No, the
Holy Spirit is not a dove, it is a fire, a man eating fire which
clamps its talons into the very crown of saints, martyrs, and
great strugglers, reducing them to ashes. Abject souls are the
ones who take the Holy Spirit for a dove which they imagine
they can kill and eat.*

NIKOS KAZANTZAKIS, REPORT TO GRECO

Subvert is one of my favorite words. It is the combination of
two Latin words: *sub* (meaning "under") and *vertere* (meaning "to
turn"). *Subvert* means to turn under, to turn upside down, to
overturn, to overthrow. A good picture of subversion is what a
plow does to soil: it turns it over, letting the good soil emerge
from beneath the surface into the sunlight.

In the beginning, we find the Spirit hovering over the unformed. While not explicit, I assume that the Spirit has a hand in bringing forth the light—the first spark of creation. We know what happens later in Genesis: innocence lost, murder, the deepening of human frailty and wickedness.

And it is into this world that the Spirit, almost behind the scenes, does her work—the work of divine re-creation. It is the Spirit who opens up new possibilities, new opportunities for God's people to be restored and transformed. Where things fall apart, and the world skews wicked, the Spirit subverts.

The Spirit brings new possibilities to light. The Spirit disrupts the status quo. The Spirit refuses to take the world as it is and instead flips it. The Spirit speaks into our reality, giving us eyes to see things as they are, so that we can deconstruct the world around us and embrace new realities.

The Spirit refuses to accept things as they are and instead woos us down the dangerous path of restoration, re-creation, renovation. We see this throughout the Hebrew Scriptures. Every time God brings about change, the Spirit is present to open eyes, inspire wisdom, reveal forgotten or new truths. It is by the power and influence of the Spirit that we have the great craftsmen and artists shaping great works (Exodus 31:2-5). It is with the voice of the Spirit that the prophets speak and challenge God's people to be faithful (2 Samuel 23). And we are told that it is through the power of this Spirit that things will be made right; justice will come to the nations (Isaiah 42).

Without the Spirit, we cannot encounter God. It is this Spirit who opens our eyes to see the world-as-it-might-be. It is this Spirit that opens our eyes to see the God-who-is-coming. It is this Spirit who then empowers us to overturn the world as it is. The Spirit subverts.

When we first encounter the Spirit in the Gospels, we see her preparing the way for the Messiah. It is the Spirit who overshadows

Mary at conception, it is the Spirit who empowers John to be the greatest prophet and it is the Spirit who anoints Jesus at his baptism.

The Spirit brings forth the Christ and then leads him into the desert to be confronted by Satan. From there, we see that Jesus' understanding of his own ministry is tied up with the Spirit, for it is the Spirit's anointing that empowers Jesus to preach good news to the poor.

And it is the Spirit who, after Jesus ascends to the Father, is unleashed upon the disciples—a terrifying wind that leaves flames dancing upon their heads. By the Spirit's power, these disciples start to vomit strange words—a terrifying sign of new unity. A great reversal of Babel, where God fragmented human speech into many languages, so that people would scatter. At Pentecost, the fragmented are brought back together.

In Luke 4, Jesus proclaims his Spirit-filled manifesto. Luke and Acts are companion volumes. They are to be read together. In volume one, Jesus is filled with the Spirit at his baptism on the edge of society and then marches to Jerusalem for a final confrontation. In volume two, the followers of Jesus are baptized with the Holy Spirit in Jerusalem and then driven to the edges of the world. The first baptism of Jesus inaugurates the Jubilee. The second baptism, at Pentecost, fulfills it.

In Acts 2, we see the disciples sharing all good things, breaking bread, praying and listening to apostolic teaching. They too, as the Spirit compels, proclaim good news to the poor, set people free from social exclusion, heal the sick, cast out demons and give sight to the blind.

It is the Spirit who collapses the distance between people. It is the Spirit who opens our eyes to the reality of God. It is the Spirit who drives us into the wild places. It is the Spirit who brings the Jubilee.

But the Spirit not only creates but also destroys. Gone are the old divisions. At Pentecost, the Spirit destroys national distinctions. And later, as the Spirit woos the Gentiles, she destroys the division between Jews and Gentiles.

And every time we see the disciples do a miraculous deed or utter a bold word, it is the Spirit who enables them to do so. Every missional step forward in the book of Acts is at the Spirit's urging. There is no mission apart from the Spirit.

The Spirit isn't a snake that can be charmed. The Spirit blows where she will. She is never commanded, never used. She is unpredictable and mysterious. She is a dangerous bird. She subverts. And when she burns in your heart, she destroys you from within, so that a new life will rise from the ashes.

The Spirit has quietly ripped apart the old world and is bringing forth the new. Within us. Let us listen to the Spirit.

A CRISIS OF IDENTITY

As we let go of our blueprints in the presence of the feral God and embrace the way of compassion, the temptation is to quickly move forward to draft a new blueprint. At the same time, we are tempted to either distance ourselves from the pain around us or, like so many before us, allow our hearts to grow numb. When I am in that place—armed with a clever plan and cut off from the depths of humanity around me—it is almost impossible for me to participate with the Spirit. I say "almost" because the Spirit still finds a way to wake me from the slumber of my own power.

Relationships are dynamic, not static. Relationships that become static fall apart. Anyone who has been in a long-term relationship understands this. In this way, we are never done repenting, turning away from those things that nurture distance, abstraction and alienation. We are never finished in our task of moving more deeply into the love of God.

This is a book about repentance. Repenting not only means turning away, letting go of those myths and things that encumber love; it is also about paying attention to the world with eyes of compassion. And then acting.

The previous two chapters explored the postures that help us to see the world differently, to see one another differently, to see God differently. I wrote about the wild undoing that is the feral God. And I wrote about the compassionate way of Jesus. Now I will turn to our role in participating with the subversion of the Spirit.

This participation requires discernment. It would be unwise to leap into the world, seeking to change it, without discerning our way forward.

Our inability to discern has fostered an identity crisis in the church. The church does not know what it is. It is pulled between the way of empire and the way of Jesus. That crisis has come from a failure to discern. Our vision has been co-opted. For many of us, we are so enamored with the American dream that it is nearly impossible to see the unkingdom of God. Nevertheless, we continue enacting bold plans. We invest billions on ministry schemes. We go around the world, sowing the seeds of faith. All the while, we assume that we are doing the work of the Spirit. Yet rarely do we stop to listen, to discern together the way the Spirit would have us act.

At best, failing to discern the leading of the Spirit results in a massive waste of resources as we forge ahead with our spiritless agendas. At worst, it has disastrous results to those experiencing oppression. How many have experienced pain as a result of the well-intentioned actions of the presumed faithful?

Christians in the so-called First World are continually presented with the temptation to, upon acquiring radical insights, go out and "try to change the world." They assume the strength of those insights will leave a deeper footprint then the hidden, unquestioned assumptions that bear the weight of Christian imperialism. We go into the world, relying upon the fruits of imperialism—formal education, wealth, entrepreneurial skills—to "bring the kingdom."

Subverting Missio Dei

In 2003, my wife and I set out to form an urban church called Missio Dei. I was a seminary student with bold and radical ideas. Or so I thought. We went through training, raised a bunch of money and launched a hip urban worship service. In that first year, I raised and spent roughly $50,000.

A year into things, things were going *okay*. We had as many attendees as could generally be expected for a new urban church—about forty or so people. But few, if any, actually lived in the city; they commuted in from the suburbs. And all of the money was basically going to pay my salary and pay the rent for a once-a-week worship space. I felt like a fraud. This wasn't the way of Jesus.

So I did what anyone probably should do in my situation. I quit. I said I was done being a pastor. I sat down with everyone who considered Missio Dei their church and told them, "My job right now as your pastor is to help you find a new church."

It sucked. My wife and I started sliding into the sort of debt one incurs when having school expenses, a mortgage and no job.

We decided to have a retreat for the few folks who wanted to discern what would come next. We met in a cheap cabin in Wisconsin. My wife and I were joined with a handful of folks who really had nowhere else to go. Several of them just happened to be living at our house at that time; they had received hospitality and just wanted to be a part of what, if anything, would come next.

I immediately started going into planning mode, but every time I started going down that road, it felt hollow. I had just lost my dream church because my plans hadn't worked. I knew in my soul that I needed to shut up. Together, we needed to listen.

I wish I could remember what it was that shifted the conversation. But as eight of us gathered in a cabin in rural Wisconsin, something shifted. We decided to center our lives around hospitality, simplicity and prayer. It didn't seem heroic or even exciting at the time. It just felt faithful. The following eight years were tremendously difficult and amazingly clarifying. We began to cultivate the practice of communal discernment.

PRACTICES FOR DISCERNING THE SUBVERSIVE SPIRIT

We still have a long way to go, but I've learned some things about listening to the Spirit together as a community. I'd like to share several of the practices that we've found particularly helpful. Again, this list isn't exhaustive. There are others that may be much more helpful to you and your community. Yet I offer what I've experienced in hope that it might serve you. It might also be helpful to dismiss the idea that discernment is a way of receiving marching orders from a sky general or a blueprint from the divine architect. God's will is more like an invitation to life than anything else. And it is ongoing. It isn't a mechanistic process of discovering God's will and then executing that will.

Practice one: open worship. I'm immensely indebted to the Quaker tradition for teaching me about discernment. I'm also indebted to the work of John Howard Yoder. His book *Body Politics* is an amazing primer for church practices. There is one practice that he calls "the Rule of Paul" (and most Quakers call "open worship"). Drawing from 1 Corinthians 14, the Rule of Paul invites those gathered to speak as led by the Holy Spirit. When finished, the speaker is to yield the floor to the next speaker. Yoder suggests that "consensus arises uncoerced out of open conversation. There is no voting in which a majority overruns a minority and no decision of a leader by virtue of his office."[1]

The Rule of Paul is, basically, that everyone is given the floor as they feel led by the Holy Spirit. And any decisions that are to be made are by consensus. This is considered impractical by many—particularly when involving an important decision. As difficult as it can sometimes be, our community has practiced open worship in one form or another for eight years, and we've never had a decision-making crisis.

At the Mennonite Worker (formerly Missio Dei), we practice the Rule of Paul in two different contexts. Often, we gather on Saturday mornings to discern through issues facing our community. In this meeting we encourage folks to speak even if they aren't sure they are being led by the Spirit. We want everyone's voice to be heard if it is a matter that they care about. There is a good deal of discussion. A facilitator is designated to make sure everyone gets a chance to speak. The facilitator also calls us to times of silence or prayer when we're "stuck."

We also set aside at least twenty minutes during our Sunday evening worship gathering to listen together in silence. In this meeting, folks are encourage to speak (or sing) if the Spirit stirs. Decision making need not be the goal. We want to listen to the Holy Spirit, rather than simply reading about how the Holy Spirit communicated to dead apostles. In a noisy world of overinformation, communal discernment is more essential than ever. Taking time to sit in silence together as we calm our thoughts and allow the Spirit to move in us is important. It is important even if nothing is said. For even the silence communicates the possibility of God moving us beyond our best plans as we wait together for a new world.

Practice two: naming and resisting. One of the five core values of the Mennonite Worker is "resistance" (the others are hospitality, simplicity, prayer and peacemaking). Often, folks ask me, "Why do you include resistance? Isn't it enough to be *for* something? Why do you need to be *against* something?" Repentance requires both a turning *from* and a turning *toward*. We are called to struggle against the principalities and powers as we seek to walk in the way of Jesus. Like the story of the Zen master (which I told in the chapter "Repenting of Christianity") how are we going to learn the way of Jesus if we don't empty our cups first? This emptying begins with naming the principalities and powers around us—by naming the myths that we've discovered. And, from there, we discern a tangible way of resisting.

I've found the following questions to be an important way of naming and resisting the principalities and powers:

1. What is a great evil or injustice we (or our friends) are experiencing in society?

2. What lies or myths do people believe that keep this injustice from being challenged?

3. What is the clearest expression of that evil or injustice? The goal is to name not the worst expression but the clearest.

4. How do we currently relate to that injustice or evil? How do we relate to that expression?

After deeply exploring these questions, we can move to the next questions in a posture of discernment:

5. Is there anything we can do to confront that expression?

6. Is there anything we can do to expose those myths or lies?

For example, Dr. King may have suggested that racism is the greatest injustice he and his friends were experiencing in society. One of the powerful myths in the civil-rights era was the myth of "separate but equal." Racism took (and takes) many forms. But the clearest expressions of racism in the civil-rights era was segregation, which was demonstrated with separate drinking fountains, separate schools, whites-only establishments, whites-only seating sections on public buses and so forth. Organizers confronted that segregation with tactics like the Montgomery Bus Boycott or lunch counter sit-ins.

Of course, the example I'm giving involves a marginalized group (African Americans) resisting oppression. Things get trickier when those of the dominant group or class attempt to confront injustice.

There is a danger of doing resistance without being attentive to our own complicity with the very thing we're trying to resist. It is important, particularly with justice work, to work on our own identities and cultivate a practice of compassion before we jump in to address societal injustice.

Practice three: arguing with Jesus. This may seem like a strange suggestion, but it has changed my relationship with Jesus. In most relationships, a lack of honesty creates a barrier to vulnerability. This seems obvious. Nevertheless, I've met so many people who are unwilling to be honest about their struggles with Jesus. One of the things we did when our community "started over" was to ask a few questions when we were studying Scripture together:

1. As we read this passage, what within us is rising up in opposition? What do we hate about it? What confuses us?

2. As we sit in the anxiety and tension raised by this passage, what may the Spirit be inviting us to reconsider about the passage?

3. Are we being invited to let go of something that is getting in the way of our ability to love?

These questions are particularly powerful when paired with the questions raised earlier (see "Practice one: experimenting with God").

If we are going to be people who are led by the Spirit in the way of Jesus, we need to be honest with ourselves. Pretenses must fall. By being honest as we read Scripture together, we give space for the Holy Spirit to move among us. The goal here is not to simply conform to what the Scripture says. We must yield our hearts to the Spirit until we are able to move forward in the love of God and neighbor. The Spirit desires our participation in re-creation, not our mere obedience.

◆   ◆   ◆

These practices aren't complete. I share them together because I believe that open worship, or something like it, is an excellent context for group spiritual discernment. And in that context, we can grapple with the positive vision of Jesus while we also grapple with the influences of the principalities and powers.

As we honestly encounter the way of Jesus and honestly engage the injustices in our society, we can begin to discern a way forward together. My hope and prayer for those reading this book is that this discernment is rooted in compassion and in the wild freedom of a God who calls us to embrace the fullness of life.

MANIFESTO (LUKE 4:18-19)

Drawing in the hot breath of God,
My shaking lungs sting,
Struggling to contain the power of the Almighty.
So I exhale the God-breath
Upon those awaiting salvation.
Prophesying powerful portents of liberation.
Awakening the imaginations of the dispossessed.
This is my manifesto:
"This is your day, pauper.
Your empty stomachs will be filled with justice
Your thirsty pockets will be quenched with peace.
The Heavenly Banker stocks your account
With cash stolen from the money changers.
No more hanging your head low.
No more thrift store spirituality.
You are the princes of the kingdom.
Freedom is yours, prisoner.
Your cell bars will turn to noodles.
You'll exchange the dank dark for golden sunsets.
The New Warden has signed your parole papers
And put the old wardens behind bars.
No more scratching the days into brick walls.
No more false religion shutting out the stars.
Now you sleep under the rising red moon.
Open your eyes, blind man.
The darkness will be choked by light.
Confusion broken by the sound of a trumpet.
The Holy Physician shows you a new world
While the watchmen are lost in the fog.

No more rubbing your eyes in despair.

No more stumbling in perpetual night.

You will bear witness to the edges of the world.

Step out of the shadows, oppressed.

The principalities will lose their thrones.

The powers will fall to earth.

The Spirit of God has ended this occupation

While the imperial fleet burns to ash and drifts away.

No more plotting impotent rebellions.

No more struggling against steel and flesh.

For you are free citizens of a new nation.

The old fires have been suffocated

While holy coals smolder,

Purifying the hearts of the people.

I announce the Jubilee upon those shivering in fear.

Shouting a sermon of shalom

As dawn of the first day breaks upon those he loves."

Ten

Jesus and the Jubilee

Affluence creates poverty.

MARSHALL McLUHAN

In 2011, as the recession marched on, people began to take to the streets around the United States (and around the world) to challenge the wealthiest 1 percent—and for good reason. People were beginning to realize that corporations rule the world. Corporations are committed to securing profits, not to securing justice.

And so, our world seems to be near the brink. The US economy is suffering, but the poor and the middle class are experiencing most of that suffering. The wealthy are somehow, through it all, continuing to maintain their wealth.

Since most USAmerican Christians separate faith from politics and economics, the church, for the most part, isn't involved in the protests.

What does the way of Jesus have to do with economic discontent? Apparently not much. Christianity may be known for its charity, but it is rarely accused of being prophetic.

At a recent Occupy Minnesota rally, the clearest example of a

Christian was a man wearing a poster board calling the protesters to "repent." With megaphone in hand, he spoke words of condemnation. He even wore a nifty red hat printed with the words "Cover Your Breasts." In a crowd filled with the discontent, the unemployed and the desperate—those struggling against a society that has been enslaved by corporate greed, this man's biggest concern was uncovered breasts.

I don't want to pick on Christians too much. After all, most people in our society don't believe an alternative is possible. We are unable to imagine a society where there are no poor or where there are no rich. Even if we could imagine such a society, would we really be interested in living in it?

We are all subject to what psychologist Bruce Levine calls "zombification"[1]—where we are largely hypnotized by television, by advertisement, by bureaucracy. We have a diminished capacity to get upset. We are lulled into a sense of false comfort.

As long as we can get enough to eat (no matter where the food comes from), can watch our favorite shows, can log into our Facebook and have a roof over our heads, most of us are content—at least content enough to stay invested in the way things are.

Among the many things that our society excels at, few rival our penchant for buying and selling. Ours is a consumer culture. We are constantly bombarded with an ever-increasing array of stuff. And we are conditioned by it. Shopping is a sacrament. We have been raised with an intense awareness that we lack. Our lives are spent, in USAmerica, trying to buy ourselves whole.

This wayward attempt to satisfy our culturally conditioned greed has resulted in environmental degradation, oil wars and social noise. But it has also resulted in spiritual vapidity.

Meanwhile, people are fragmented; more than ever, they are being pulled into too many directions to feel satisfied. We are stressed and lonely and tired. But instead of seeking a radically different way of life, we seem to cure our overconsumption by adding more to the shopping cart of life.

And so we find ourselves with an overdeveloped sense of lack. We are encouraged to shop and surf our way to wholeness. Even spirituality—which should be our way out of this trap—has largely been repackaged and digitized for easy consumption.

But it doesn't have to be this way.

THOSE HOLY HIPPIES

The early church was like a hippie commune, but without all of the sex. Well, I'm sure some people had sex, but they were probably married.

According to the book of Acts, "All the believers were one in heart and mind. No one claimed that any of their possessions was their own, but they shared everything they had. . . . And God's grace was so powerfully at work in them all that there were no needy persons among them" (Acts 4:32-34).

This sounds nice, doesn't it? Can you imagine being a part of a group of one heart and mind, where you love each other so much that you meet all one another's needs?

Isn't this what we spend our whole lives trying to achieve? We work hard to have enough money to take care of all of our needs, but try not to work so hard that we can't share our life with those we love.

How is that working for you?

Sometimes you'll find a family that experiences something like this, but can you imagine an entire movement of people—many who were once strangers, from diverse social and economic backgrounds—living like this?

Neither can I. But it was Jesus' vision for his movement. And it meant that everyone had to share.

Let's unpack Jesus' vision a bit more:

A certain ruler asked him, "Good teacher, what must I do to inherit eternal life?"

"Why do you call me good?" Jesus answered. "No one is good—except God alone. You know the commandments: 'You shall not commit adultery, you shall not murder, you shall not steal, you shall not give false testimony, honor your father and mother.'"

"All these I have kept since I was a boy," he said.

When Jesus heard this, he said to him, "You still lack one thing. Sell everything you have and give to the poor, and you will have treasure in heaven. Then come, follow me."

When he heard this, he became very sad, because he was very wealthy. Jesus looked at him and said, "How hard it is for the rich to enter the kingdom of God! Indeed, it is easier for a camel to go through the eye of a needle than for someone who is rich to enter the kingdom of God." (Luke 18:18-25)

If I had a "top five most dismissed passages of the New Testament" list, this passage would make it. In fact, I have yet to meet a wealthy person who feels it applies to them.

Most folks dismiss this passage by suggesting that Jesus knew the rich young ruler's heart and knew that he had a personal problem with wealth, which, thankfully, isn't really such a problem among twenty-first-century American Christians. This logic assumes that the rich man's wealth is incidental—Luke could just of easily written about the angry young ruler, or perhaps the cursing young ruler. In the case of the latter, the young cusser would have become sad, because he was very cursey. Jesus would then look at him and say "How hard is it for the potty-mouthed to enter the kingdom of God!"

Unfortunately, this doesn't work. The Gospel of Luke talks about wealth and poverty—a lot. Jesus tells not only the rich young ruler to sell everything but also his disciples. In Luke 12:32-33, Jesus tells his followers: "Do not be afraid, little flock, for your Father has been pleased to give you the kingdom. Sell your possessions and give to the poor. Provide purses for yourselves that will not wear out, a treasure in heaven that will never fail, where no thief comes near and no moth destroys." Jesus' concerns about wealth extended much further than one rich young ruler.

In fact, in Jesus' inaugural address—the first sermon he gives in his public ministry—he essentially proclaims that Jubilee has come:

> "The Spirit of the Lord is on me,
>> because he has anointed me
>> to proclaim good news to the poor.
> He has sent me to proclaim freedom for the prisoners
>> and recovery of sight for the blind,
> to set the oppressed free,
>> to proclaim the year of the Lord's favor."
> Then he rolled up the scroll, gave it back to the attendant
> and sat down. The eyes of everyone in the synagogue
> were fastened on him. He began by saying to them,
> "Today this scripture is fulfilled in your hearing." (Luke
>> 4:18-21)

Many scholars agree that "the year of the Lord's favor"—which is found originally in Isaiah 61—is referring to the institution of the Jubilee.

According to the Hebrew Jubilee (which at the very least informed Jesus' approach to economics), if someone has amassed wealth, it doesn't *necessarily* matter if it is directly at the expense of the poor. Hoarding would be seen as *intrinsically* stealing from the poor. And, as such, it would have been unjust. Take a look at Leviticus 25 to read more on what God was going for with the Jubilee: it meant a canceling of all debts, a return of land to their previous occupants and an end to all slavery. It was liberation. It was a great big sociopolitical CTRL+ALT+DELETE. It was a rebooting of the system—an end to injustice.

But Jesus wasn't asking Israel to start practicing Jubilee every fifty years. Instead, as acclaimed biblical scholar N. T. Wright suggests, Jesus was using Jubilee language in this passage to point to an ongoing practice that, rather than being practiced once every fifty years by Israel, was to be practiced in continuity by the disciples.[2]

An honest reading of Luke-Acts lays this out. The early church lived like a bunch of Jesus-loving hippies. Nevertheless, whenever I talk to folks about Jesus' call to Jubilee, people push back—especially if they have money. The modern USAmerican understanding of justice is quite different than the justice of Jesus. Nowhere can we find in his Jubilee vision that a wealthy person needs only to give alms to be justified, since wealth comes from the land, and the land, which ultimately belongs to God, is granted to his people. In light of this, the call of the wealthy isn't simply to be charitable. Charity doesn't get at justice. Even when Jubilee ceases to be rooted in the Promised Land, it is still assumed that, in Christ, everything belongs to the Lord and should, therefore, be redistributed to those in need as an act of justice—not as an act of "charity."

In other words, Jesus never intended for some of his followers to be wealthy while others remained poor.

And, in the beginning, it seems that the church actually practiced Jubilee. In the early chapters of Acts, we see a church where all of the needs are met. Folks would sell everything they had and share the proceeds to care for one another. They didn't see it as an act of charity—charity accepts the status quo. When we do charity, we give out of our affluence to help the poor; we don't actually sacrifice our affluence to destroy the distinction between the rich and the poor.

No, the early church wasn't charitable. They were revolutionary. They lived, for a short time, in Jubilee.

When we love each other, we share all good things with one another. Love applied to economics is Jubilee. Love means risking one's economic security to share. When Jesus spoke of money, he didn't challenge the wealthy because they were mean to poor people. Rather, he challenged them because they put their own security above the needs of their neighbors.

And so, the challenge to the "rich young ruler" wasn't to start being charitable, but to remove the very thing that divided him from his poor sisters and brothers—his wealth. By selling everything he had, he could purchase kinship with the poor and thus be a part with them in the unkingdom of God. And this is our challenge as well.

In Luke 6:20, Jesus says, "Blessed are you who are poor, for yours is the kingdom." The unkingdom of God is for the poor. And, impossibly, it is for the rich who practice Jubilee by sharing all good things with the poor.

But sharing all good things with the poor isn't a heroic act. We don't earn an extra jewel in our heaven-crowns for it. It is simply the most human thing we can do. It is a simple and honest act of love.

We often use Jesus as an example of downward mobility. It is assumed that, in heaven, Jesus was kind of wealthy, and that he left that all behind to slum it with the poor folks. But Jesus isn't simply someone who decided to serve the poor. He was poor. He didn't speak as the affluent who advocates for the poor; he spoke as a representative of the poor. I wonder if, to Jesus, it was a greater temptation to look down on the poor or the rich young ruler. Perhaps he looks at everyone the same—but maybe he had more pity for the rich young ruler than he did for the poor lepers he sometimes healed.

Whether Jesus addressed the wealthy or the poor, his goal was to call folks into a righteous relationship with God and neighbor. Jesus' sermons and acts serve to convert the marginalized into human beings. His are acts of liberation for the oppressed and the poor.

But what of the rich and the powerful? In this encounter with the rich young ruler, we see the way that they are to enter into the unkingdom. They also need to be converted into human beings.

If the poor become marginalized and dehumanized because of oppressive power and the crushing weight of social, economic and religious systems, then the ones who wield that power and create or support those systems also become dehumanized, but in a different way.

In fact, if you read through Luke-Acts carefully, it becomes apparent that Luke isn't simply rejecting the wealthy (it is valid to believe that Luke himself was wealthy at some point) but is instead deeply interested in the salvation of the wealthy.

But let's get practical. What is, ultimately, the goal of the wealthy divesting of their wealth? The goal is to share possessions, which is what we see in the early chapters of Acts. When wealthy people come to faith, they are to share everything with the poor, who receive it. But the poor and the wealthy don't then go their separate ways; rather, they live as family. The goal of downward mobility isn't mere charity, but solidarity.

Thus, Jesus opens for us an economic vision that destroys the economic divisions between people. It is a vision that is firmly within our reach. It doesn't require an overhaul of the "system." It simply requires that a group of people live like family across class lines. Simple, right?

OF JUBILEES AND GUMMY BEARS
One night about five years ago, we were finishing a Wednesday community meal. On this particular night, there were probably a dozen people gathered around the table. We were feeling good, and we didn't want the night to end.

"Let's go to a movie!" someone suggested.

Within minutes, an outing was planned.

At this point it might be worth mentioning that I have two major weaknesses (well, more than two, but I'm only going to share two with you right now): gummy bears and movies. I will never say no to either. My mind is a sad sponge, having absorbed thousands of meaningless film hours. And my body is a sad sponge as well—having absorbed hundreds of pounds of gummies.

One day when my wife was out of town visiting her parents, I ate a five-pound bag of gummy bears. And I'd do it again.

On this particular occasion, I'm not sure what movie we saw. I've seen thousands of movies. I don't really remember who went on the outing either. I can only be certain of two things:

1. I ate gummies at the movie.

2. "Don" wasn't there.

Over the eight years thus far of the Mennonite Worker's existence, we've received dozens of guests. Don (not his real name) stands out as a guest for a number of reasons. He had lost his apartment because he lost his job. He lost his job because he was no longer able to work. He was unable to work because his chemotherapy made him weak. And on top of all of that, he was HIV-positive.

Don was one of the warmest, kindest guests we've ever had.

That night Don wasn't at the movie because he didn't have money to go to the movie. I suppose I could have bought him a ticket, but that would have meant not getting gummy bears.

I can be an idiot sometimes.

◆　◆　◆

The truth is, in many small and large ways, we do the same thing every day. It usually comes down to a choice between having more for ourselves or sharing what we have with others.

To Jesus, mammon (which is an interesting Aramaic word that is perhaps best translated as "wealth") is like a false god who woos away the rich and keeps them from being in community with the people of God. And it is a force that enslaves the poor, keeping them from awaking to their full humanity. Mammon isn't a neutral thing—it is a perilous tool that can either purchase solidarity or serve as a wall dividing the wealthy from the poor.

Jesus doesn't say, "Where your heart is, there is your treasure," he says, "Where your treasure is, there is your heart." The difference is important.

Let me put it this way: Jesus says that our hearts follow after our treasure like a dog runs after a stick. How we spend our money (or our resources) determines where our heart will be—what kind of a person we'll be. There is, at least in Jesus' teachings, no such thing as a hoarder whose heart is with the poor. Solidarity isn't a sentiment.

So, like the rich young ruler, we USAmericans are being asked to use our wealth to embrace Jubilee. We are being invited to participate in the sort of society that looks like a family, where we are of one heart and one mind, and where no one is needy.

Eleven

Jesus and the Revolutionary Table

Love casts out fear, but we have to get over the fear
in order to get close enough to love them.

DOROTHY DAY

On Saturdays, we used to gather at the empty lot across from Palmer's Bar to serve vegan chili to the neighborhood. We called this weekly ritual the Hospitality Train—the line of bicycles hauling trailers filled with a propane burner, buckets (to be used as chairs), a canopy, a large pot, serving utensils and so forth reminded us of a train.

One day, I was taking a break from the Hospitality Train; I was walking down Cedar Avenue to get a soda from West Bank Grocery—one of the small Somali-owned groceries in the area. As I walked, I noticed a man on the far end of the block walking toward me. Even from the distance, I sensed he was homeless; he was clothed with too many layers for a warm day and was hauling a large backpack.

As he got closer, I saw that he walked with a heavy limp. He was wearing glasses with one lens blacked out. And he was looking at me with a smile on his face.

It seemed likely that he was going to ask me for money. Usually, when a homeless man asks for money, it comes with some sort of story. Interestingly, these stories often sound the same. There is the classic, "I need money for gas because my car broke down a few miles away," or "I need money for the bus to visit my sick wife (or child)." Sometimes the story is more elaborate, offering a rapid-fire account of all the miseries in life that my two dollars can help alleviate.

Often in those cases, I'd feel a mixture of sympathy and frustration. I'd feel sympathetic because most people end up on the streets for legitimately sad reasons. Few people choose homelessness for happy reasons. But I'd also feel frustration because I didn't like the feeling of doubting someone's story. I wanted to live in a world where folks told the truth.

As this man walked toward me on the sidewalk, I began to feel that helpless combination of sympathy and frustration. I started to wonder what sort of story he'd tell me and what sort of response I might give that could strike the perfect balance between compassion and frugality.

As my mind pondered these things, I suddenly felt God's presence, along with the words "give him whatever he asks for."

I didn't have time to think things over before the man stopped and asked: "Can I have five dollars?"

I was stunned. I'm not sure which surprised me more—that God had decided to speak into my mind or that this man had simply asked for money without an accompanying story.

I was so surprised that I responded with untypical candor: "Good thing you didn't ask for a hundred!"

The man just looked at me, confused.

"As I saw you walking toward me, I felt God tell me to give you whatever you asked for, so thank you for just asking for five bucks," I said, smiling.

Upon hearing my explanation, he took off his backpack and removed a wirebound notebook. With excitement, he shared a couple of his poems, which he had written to Jesus.

That was how I became friends with Michael.

I'd like to tell you that we lived happily ever after. But in the years since that mystical encounter on the street—where God spoke into my experience and tore down, if only for a few minutes, the walls of separation between Michael and me—we have caused each other a great deal of pain.

In the few weeks following that first meeting, I came to learn a bit of Michael's difficult story. I learned of his history of abuse and his time in and out of jail. At the time, Michael was in his mid-fifties. He had spent a significant part of his adulthood on the streets. A lot of that had to do with his addictions, which mostly served as a way of medicating psychological and physical pain.

During those first few weeks, he started calling me "big brother." He'd announce me to strangers that way: "Hey, this is my big brother Mark." This was strange for several reasons. Not only was he twenty years my senior, he was also a good nine inches shorter than me. And he was black and I am white.

I began to call him my brother too. I even started ending conversations with "I love you, brother." Now, that may seem like a small thing to you. But for some men (like me) who've been shaped by the sort of emotionally repressive stoic culture of rural Minnesota, it was a big deal. To this day, I've probably only said "I love you" to fewer than ten people.

Then, one day, Michael asked if he could crash at our house for a few days. This wasn't an unexpected request. At that time, my wife and I were living with a few others from the Mennonite

Worker. We had decided to maintain a guest room for folks in need of lodging. I assumed it would be fine. But I told him I needed to check with my housemates first.

There were six people living in our house at that time. Five agreed to extend hospitality to Michael. One refused. And, since we had agreed to make these sorts of decisions by consensus, I had to tell Michael that he wasn't welcome in my home.

I was hurt and angry. I felt like a hypocrite—here I was, calling a man "brother" and I couldn't even let him sleep on a couch for a few days.

Michael took the rejection relatively well, I thought. I thought to myself, *he's homeless; he's probably used to this sort of thing.*

That evening, he hit the bottle hard and was picked up by the police for a "drunken disorderly" charge. Since it was a violation of his probation, he went to jail for a year.

It was one of the worst nights of my life. I remember screaming and crying into my pillow as my wife feebly tried to console me. I felt like a hypocrite—I said one thing yet did another. My treatment of Michael, as reasonable as it may seem to so many people, felt like a betrayal of the gospel.

A COOTIE INFESTATION

It is easy to exclude people; we do it all the time. Often, we have little reason. Sometimes our exclusion is based upon national borders or ethnic identities. Sometimes it is because of religion. Perhaps they just look strange and make us feel uncomfortable. In the case of Michael, we excluded him because he was a homeless black man. When we exclude someone simply because they are a certain type of person, that is called *sociomoral disgust.* Psychologist Richard Beck writes:

> In sociomoral disgust people and entire populations can be seen as sources of contamination. Thus, contact with these

persons can elicit the strong revulsion of the disgust response.
. . . Sociomoral disgust can extend, on a case-by-case basis, to
individuals we deem "disgusting," "revolting," or "creepy."
We make these attributions for a variety of reasons (e.g., poor
hygiene, moral failures). Regardless as to the source of the
attribution, we experience feelings of revulsion in proximity
to these people . . . sociomoral disgust can [also apply] to
entire populations. . . . Wherever hate, racism, or genocidal
impulses exist, sociomoral contamination and disgust take
center stage.[1]

You'd think that first-century Israel had a cootie infestation. In
child lore, cooties is a sort of imaginative infectious disease—a way
of marking off those kids who should be excluded for a variety of
reasons. What seems relatively "harmless" on a playground becomes absolutely wicked at the sociopolitical level.

The Pharisees maintained a system of social exclusion. Of
course, Romans and other Gentiles were off limits. But even fellow
Jews labeled "sinners" and "tax collectors" certainly had cooties.
These weren't simply people to be avoided for their bad influence;
they were labeled "unclean." It was a way of ritualizing and spiritualizing exclusion.

In his book *Unclean*, Dr. Beck makes the case that Jesus' words
and actions directly challenged the way in which sociomoral
disgust operated in his society. In Matthew 9:9-13, we read:

As Jesus went on from there, he saw a man named Matthew
sitting at the tax collector's booth. "Follow me," he told him,
and Matthew got up and followed him.

While Jesus was having dinner at Matthew's house, many
tax collectors and sinners came and ate with him and his disciples. When the Pharisees saw this, they asked his disciples,
"Why does your teacher eat with tax collectors and sinners?"

On hearing this, Jesus said, "It is not the healthy who need a doctor, but the sick. But go and learn what this means: 'I desire mercy, not sacrifice.' For I have not come to call the righteous, but sinners."

Throughout the Gospels, Jesus offends the Pharisees with the company he keeps. To the Pharisees, holiness was maintained by excluding the unclean. Jesus smashed their notions of holiness. It was a big no-no to be a guest in the home of a disreputable person. It still is today, but even more so back then. Few things were more upsetting to the religious establishment of Jesus' day than who he ate with. He ate with tax collectors—who were considered national traitors and religious rejects. He ate with prostitutes. He ate with "sinners" (in the New Testament, to call one a "sinner" was like calling them trash). It was much deeper than a cootie violation. Jesus was including folks who were traitors; he was including folks who were immoral. And by sitting at table with them, it was assumed he was contaminated by them.

But Jesus' offense goes much deeper than that. In Matthew 8:1-4, an unclean man, a leper, comes before Jesus, begging to be healed and saying, "Lord, if you are willing, you can make me clean." Jesus reaches out and touches him (thus making himself ceremonially unclean) and only *then* heals him. Jesus was willing to make himself unclean before he cleansed others. We see this throughout the Gospels: Jesus associates with sinners before they fully leave their sin behind. He meets them where they are at in order to call them. He doesn't stand outside of their lives, calling them out, waiting for them to get their act together before he'll embrace them. We should be grateful for this; otherwise we'd all be left on our own.

Jesus' actions weren't merely compassionate. They were destructive to the fabric of his society. He was willing to transgress social boundaries wherever he found them.

Let's go back to Jesus' words in Matthew 9. "It is not the healthy who need a doctor, but the sick. But go and learn what this means: '*I desire mercy, not sacrifice.*' For I have not come to call the righteous, but sinners" (emphasis added).

What is Jesus getting at here? This phrase "I desire mercy, not sacrifice" is repeated in Matthew 12 when the Pharisees got upset with Jesus and the disciples for picking grain on and healing on the sabbath.

"Sacrifice" refers to that mechanism for ritual cleansing and repentance. It is the impulse toward purity that marks off and excludes that which is not holy. It maintains the boundary between clean and unclean, holy and unholy. To show mercy, however, is about crossing purity boundaries. To show mercy is to include and embrace the "undeserving"—outsiders, the unclean, the sinner.

According to Dr. Beck, the impulses between mercy and sacrifice are "intrinsically incompatible." Jesus was forced to choose between the priestly role of maintaining purity or the prophetic role of seeking justice. To Jesus, the Pharisaic pursuit of purity alienated whole groups of people. But their fixation on purity was itself a reaction to earlier generations of religious intermingling and loose morality.

Jesus' way around this impasse wasn't simply to reject the purity impulse. Rather, he reverses it. Beck writes, "Rather than the unclean polluting the clean, we see, in Jesus' touch, the clean making the polluted pure. Here, in Jesus, we see a reversal, a *positive contamination.* Contact *cleanses* rather than pollutes."[2]

In Jesus' approach, being godly is more about who we include than who we exclude. If our first impulse is holiness, we'll set boundaries to protect ourselves. If our first impulse is mercy, we'll cross boundaries, showing love and hospitality to those who are perhaps hardest for us to love. Using the analogy of the playground, we must start spreading "good cooties" of inclusion, and we must first go to those who have most felt left out.

But few of us play the cooties game anymore. Few of us divide our social worlds into "clean" and "unclean." But we can imagine those in our society that we hold in contempt. We can imagine those people we'd feel uncomfortable sitting next to on a bus.

In my neighborhood, I have seen young, clean-cut white folks cross to the other side of the street to avoid walking too close to Somali neighbors. I've seen folks desperately avoid the homeless man with his sign (I'm guilty of that). In my younger days, I'd often go out of my way to avoid the cross-dresser who would come into the grocery store where I worked.

Pause for a moment to think about all the people who make you uncomfortable. Be honest, and take at least a few moments before continuing.

Imagine one day you come upon a group of people and you realize it includes all of the folks you tend to exclude—all of the people that make you uncomfortable. Imagine that you walk up to the group and notice, in the middle of those gathered, Jesus. He is laughing and has his arm around the shoulders of someone you'd find particularly contemptible.

Jesus included the unclean (even the ones you would exclude). With his love, they were rendered clean. And he rarely, if ever, put any conditions upon his inclusion.

THE PEOPLE OF THE TABLE

Apart from the table, the New Testament doesn't make sense. After all, Paul saved some of his harshest critiques for those who abused the common table—saying that, because of their lack of love for one another, they ate at a "table of demons" instead of the table of the Lord. And among other things, Jesus was condemned because of who he ate with. His adversaries couldn't tolerate him sullying himself by eating with "sinners." Likewise, the church was expected to practice hospitality to the stranger—to gather strangers around the table.

The posture of our way of life as the church is, in some ways, summarized by the table. The table is the place of mutuality and respect for our sisters and brothers. The table is the place where we welcome the outsider. And the table is the place for which we leave the comfort of our own home to dine with "sinners."

Hospitality is at the heart of Christianity. And, by definition, it is practiced with strangers. Sharing food and shelter and laughter with friends and family is good, but it isn't hospitality. The word *hospitality* comes from the Latin root *hospes* which means "stranger" or "guest." It can also, in some instances, mean "host." The Greek word for hospitality is *philoxenos*. This is, incidentally, the word for hospitality we find in the New Testament. *Philo-* (the first part of the word) is a prefix meaning "love" and *xenos* (the second part of the word) means "stranger," but it can also mean "host." And so, *philoxenos* can mean both "love for the stranger" and "love from the host."

In ancient Greece, practice of hospitality was tied to Zeus, the chief deity. Folks referred to him as Xenios Zeus—Zeus the Stranger—and believed that any stranger could be Zeus in disguise. This myth served to stress the utmost importance of hospitality. The hosts were to welcome strangers, wash their feet, offer food and wine, and—only after the guest was comfortable—ask the stranger's name.

These linguistic and historical tidbits point to the reality that hospitality, in its ancient sense, isn't simply about welcoming a stranger, but it is also about equalizing the guest and the host. A host who begrudgingly showed care to a guest was considered a poor host. Hosts were to treat guests as equals and help them feel comfortable before even asking their name.

The early Christians were certainly shaped by the Greco-Roman ideas of hospitality. But, just as importantly, they were shaped by Hebrew ideas as well.

In ancient Israel, it was considered the cultural norm to care for strangers and foreigners living among you. The Bible commanded as much. And when the needy and the foreigner weren't cared for, it was grounds for divine judgment.

Within the larger arc of the story of Israel, it was assumed that aliens could become faithful citizens of Israel. In a way, the ultimate hospitality of God and his people was the ability for outsiders to be included. It is, arguably, for that reason that God set Israel apart as a sign to the nations.

And so we get to the day of Jesus. Clearly, both Hebraic and Greco-Roman ideas of hospitality are influencing Jesus and the early church. But Christian hospitality seems to trump both the Hebraic and Greco-Roman notions of hospitality.

In Jesus' teachings, we go from the myth of entertaining Zeus to believing that every stranger we entertain is the same as entertaining Jesus. For example, in the chilling sheep-and-goats section of Matthew 25, Jesus reminds us "whatever you did for one of the least of these brothers and sisters of mine, you did for me" (v. 40). Jesus also broke social norms by being a guest to questionable hosts (Luke 19:1-10).

Christian hospitality is almost always radical, but it is rarely revolutionary. There is little doubt that practicing hospitality gets back to the roots of early Christian practice. But, by itself, it isn't transformative. It is important, in our doing of hospitality, that we don't embrace the conceit that, simply by feeding the hungry, housing the homeless, or giving aid to those in need, we are destroying social barriers. The world is filled with practitioners of hospitality that, even after years of charitable work, are condescending. It is relatively easy to practice hospitality without embracing justice.

If we, the church, are to be a people of hospitality—a people of welcome—we are also called to leave our places of safety to bring healing into brokenness. This way of life is clearly seen in Jesus' patterns of ministry.

If we extend hospitality with open hearts, eventually our guests and friends from the margins will become a part of our community. It is easy to minister to "them." But it is hard to be like family to those whom we judge as "less" than us. Paul knew this reality all too well—he was constantly challenging the churches throughout the empire to love one another like family. Nevertheless, the Gentiles judged the Jews and the Jews judged the Gentiles. And the wealthy disrespected the poor (though, interestingly, we don't hear about the poor disrespecting the wealthy).

The table is a place without judgment. It is a place of acceptance and mutuality. It is a place where all of us come just as we are before God to experience God's presence in and through one another. Jesus' way of hospitality goes way beyond welcome—it is transformative. The ultimate goal of hospitality is tearing down the walls of division.

This is why Paul had such strong words for the Corinthian church, essentially arguing that when we bring social divisions to our dining room table, we are eating judgment. The Eucharist—the holy meal of the gathered saints—is a revolutionary sacrament. It isn't magical—by eating bread and wine we don't simply become like Jesus. Rather, it is a place where we can reimagine our shared humanity in such a way that we can then go forth and infect the world with healing and liberation.

Around the common table, prejudices, judgments and inequities are to become undone. Hospitality provides not only an opportunity to attend to basic needs but also a chance at destroying the very inequities that render such attention necessary.

The question is, how do we embody God's heart? Can we be a people who sit at table with strangers and let the walls of division fall? Can we gather together and allow the Spirit to weave us into one new people? How do we take everything that is ours and yield it to God's dream for us? How do we welcome the stranger as Christ and be a willing guest in uncomfortable places? We must give and receive revolutionary hospitality.

Revolutionary hospitality refuses to accept the status quo. It moves beyond mere charity and instead creates space for enemies to live as family, strangers to live as friends. It challenges the assumption that some are more important than others. Celebrity and hierarchy and power-over are undone at the revolutionary table.

I believe this begins with hospitality—by inviting people into our common lives in such a way that our most basic understanding of family and community is transformed. Hospitality becomes revolutionary when the line between the host and the guest, the owner and the dispossessed, the master and the slave, the privileged and the marginalized gets so blurred that we can begin to redefine our social relations in the way of Jesus Christ.

When we gather around the table, we can experience Jesus Christ through our friends, through strangers and even through enemies. And we can begin to become the body of Christ, showing God's love to an inhospitable world.

Conclusion

When Repentance Becomes Revolution

I want to thank you for walking with me through the pages of this book. It certainly isn't a "feel good" book—at least superficially. Yet I believe there is a hope found in repentance. We never come to the end of repentance—of turning away from the old world as we step with fragility into the new. That can be a discouraging thought, because our hearts long for utopia.

But it can be a hopeful thing, knowing that there is always a deeper reality to step into. In the words of the unicorn at the end of C. S. Lewis's *Last Battle*: "I have come home at last! This is my real country! I belong here. This is the land I have been looking for all my life, though I never knew it till now. . . . Come further up, come further in!"[1] The call to repentance is our call to go further up and further into the deep reality of God.

This task is deeply mystical, intensely personal and highly political. The intermingling of these categories can raise anxiety. As I wrote this book, people would ask, "What's your book about?" Often I would say, "Well, it is a call to embrace Jesus' mystical anarchism." Such a description hardly encourages the cozy reading of books by a warm fire, with hot cocoa within easy reach.

So while this book isn't cozy, I have found writing it to be a comfort. My hope is that all of those who read this book, those who I suspect are discontent with the world as it is, may find comfort in the revolutionary provocations I've tried to articulate.

In the end, this book is an invitation to do what many radicals have dreamed of through the ages: to build a new society in the shell of the old. To build this new society requires a mystical vision wherein we believe that God can tear down the walls that imprison us. To build this new society requires new eyes and a strange willingness to be dismissed as a fool. There is a wild foolishness in embracing the unkingdom of God.

Paulo Freire suggests in *Pedagogy of the Oppressed* that whenever we act in this world in truth, we change the world. This is why mysticism and radical action must go together. To act in truth requires that we first see in truth. But to see the truth, we must first have started walking in the way of truth. There is a paradox here that can only be resolved by heeding Philip's call to "come and see" (John 1:46).

May we listen to the prophetic call to repent as we step into the mystical call to see the world with new eyes. And then, as we step into the new world (the unkingdom of God), the world is changed.

This is potentially revolutionary. According to anarchist anthropologist David Graeber:

> revolutionary action is any collective action which rejects, and therefore confronts, some form of power or domination and in doing so, reconstitutes social relations—even within the collectivity—in that light. Revolutionary action does not necessarily have to aim to topple governments. Attempts to create autonomous communities in the face of power . . . would, for instance, be almost by definition revolutionary acts. And history shows us that the continual accumulation of such acts can change (almost) everything.[2]

Revolution doesn't begin by the seizing of power, the toppling of governments or even in the rising tides of anger. It begins with love. This is how repentance becomes revolution—as we pray "God, may we give up for love's sake even what you have given us," as we walk into the new world that we are creating together with the Spirit, a new world inaugurated by Jesus Christ. This new world is the unkingdom of God.

Afterword

I've lived in my current home for a number of years, and every time I step into my backyard the squirrels dart away immediately. They fear me no matter how long I have demonstrated my commitment to nonviolence.

I see little distinction in the neurology between humans and squirrels. We ingenious human beings have the intellect of the gods, but our primitive fight-or-flight reflex demonstrates that we have the psychology of squirrels.

The logical conclusion of the survival instinct is empire. A humane society assumes live and let live, but empire is built on the logic of kill or be killed. Both the instinct to survive and the impulse to empire are driven by fear. Empires are built on enforced homogeneity in ethnicity, language, culture or geography, combined with the impulse to universalize one's particularity. Any who resists this drive to hegemony becomes the enemy of empire.

Against the various forms of fear that drove the religious establishment and political arrangements of his day, Jesus never gave in. The embodiment of humanity, he never acted out of the instinct to survive. When confronted with enemies, he turned the other cheek. When exploited, he offered all that he had. When betrayed by his closest disciples even unto death, he forgave and made them business partners. Against all the forces of fear in his time, Jesus was the model of humane love.

In contemporary psychological terms, I would argue that Jesus was a perfectly self-differentiated, nonanxious presence, which upset all kinds of family and other systems around him. Jesus taught people true humanity. As the incarnation of God he modeled a way to be humane rather than act like animals, a shepherd of the sheep in a dog-eat-dog world.

Mark Van Steenwyk rightly points out that "myths are the lies we all agree are truth." The proven path for an oppressive regime to legitimate its power is to overwhelm history with ideology. The myth of American exceptionalism rooted in the delusion of its immaculate conception is one such example. Christian denominational triumphalism is another. If, as Mark says, "abstraction begets evil," then USAmerica is particularly vulnerable as the progeny of Plato's dualism.

The way to cast this demonic ideology out is by following the flesh-and-blood Jesus of the Bible—not the plastic Jesus, the Scandinavian Jesus or the poster-child Jesus.

Empire seduces its population with the promise that every single person can be "special." This self-deception is pervasive in white America. And it's not that those who want to be special cannot love; it's that the need to be special is in direct competition with serving the interests of others.

I try my best to cast out this particular demon from my congregants with this spiel:

There are seven billion people on this earth just like you. Hardly anyone cared when you were born and hardly anyone will care when you die. No matter what you do on this earth, good or bad, most people aren't going to care because they are mostly concerned for themselves. Once you get over your heroism project and recognize that life is about living and loving and being loved, then life becomes simple and manageable. No need to strive, no need to achieve, no need to prove anything to anyone, no supremacy necessary. Loving God and loving neighbor—this is the way out of empire, this is the way into the kingdom of God.

Trusting God to provide for all of our needs means that we become liberated from self-concern. We finally have the space to pay attention to others, to pour ourselves out as an offering to God. I believe that following Jesus—this penniless, homeless, disreputable, Palestinian Jew—actually becomes the way to true human dignity. Maybe one day we'll see that when we Christians go along with the logic of empire, or prop up national exceptionalism, we debase and humiliate ourselves. Instead, the radical rejection of imperial "reality" paves the way for radical Christian living and a dignified life together.

Mark and I have been traveling companions in the Twin Cities for a number of years. I'm a third-generation Korean Presbyterian in a mainline context. Mark has a more eclectic white evangelical background. The church I lead has a steeple, paid staff and all the marks of tradition. The church Mark leads is a run-down house in the middle of the city that is experimental and cutting-edge. But what we have in common are our personal journeys that lead us to depend less and less on the systems that keep the present order entrenched. Our commitment to read the Bible plainly and to follow Jesus radically means that we expect every stone in our present temples, both secular and sacred, to be dismantled. Both of us—I in my traditional context and Mark in his unconventional one—expect the structures of empire to be thrown down because Jesus will come again to establish the unkingdom of God.

Jin S. Kim
Pastor, Church of All Nations

Acknowledgments

To Amy, whom I met the same weekend I met Jesus. I didn't walk this radical path alone; she walked with me. Her strength and compassion continue to inspire me to move more deeply into the way of Jesus.

To Jonas, my luminous little man. He appears so frequently in these pages, he deserves to be named as a coauthor.

To the Mennonite Worker, my community. Without them, I would never have left my own mind long enough to walk Jesus' radical path. I owe them all my love, but I am especially thankful to Sarah Lynne for pushing me to write better and helping me develop some of my reflections on anarchism.

To Eliacin Rosario-Cruz, my brother. We set out to write a book together, but I got distracted along the way.

To Orrin Pratt, my megaphone. He helps me find my voice.

To Joanna Shenk, my comrade. When we work together, radical stuff happens.

To Nekeisha Alexis-Baker, my coconspirator at Jesus Radicals. She has pushed me into a deeper anarchism.

To Tim Nafziger, my fellow strategist. We've spent hours talking together about what it means to live out the gospel as white men.

To Josh Bau, my culinary companion. He offered his cabin for writing getaways and, more importantly, his friendship.

To Ched Myers and Wes Howard-Brook, my intellectual mentors. They taught me how to read the Bible with radical eyes.

To Sue Ferguson Johnson, my spiritual director. She taught me to read my soul with radical eyes.

To Mark Scandrette, my sensei. He pushed me to relearn how to learn.

To David Fitch, who wrote the foreword. A shared distrust of consumerism brought us together, but our hopes for the church keep us together.

To Jin Kim, who wrote the afterword. I look forward to our future experiments into the unkingdom of God.

To my friends at the Central Plains Mennonite Conference, without whose support I would never have been free to write this book.

To David Zimmerman, my editor and friend. There was no question in my mind that he should edit this book. He has made it so much better than it was.

Notes

Introduction

[1] Quoted in Jim Cullen, *The American Dream: A Short History of an Idea That Shaped a Nation* (New York: Oxford University Press, 2003), p. 4.

1 The Gospel According to the Empire

[1] For more information, visit www.JesusRadicals.com/Iconocast.

[2] For example, Michael Hardt and Antonio Negri in their book *Empire* (Cambridge, MA: Harvard University Press, 2000).

[3] Rodney Stark, *The Rise of Christianity* (San Francisco: Harper, 1997), pp. 6-7.

[4] H. A. Drake, *Constantine and the Bishops* (Baltimore: Johns Hopkins University Press, 2002).

[5] For more on the way in which religious violence became legitimate after Constantine, see Michael Gaddis's important book, *There Is No Crime for Those Who Have Christ* (Berkeley: University of California Press, 2005).

[6] Richard Bauckham, *The Bible and Ecology* (Waco: Baylor University Press, 2010), p. 37.

[7] Ibid., p. 28.

[8] David Armitage, *The Ideological Origins of the British Empire* (Cambridge: Cambridge University Press, 2000), p. 97.

[9] Ched Myers, "To Serve and Preserve," *Sojourners* (March 2004), http://sojo.net/magazine/2004/03/serve-and-preserve.

[10] William P. Brown, *The Seven Pillars of Creation* (Oxford: Oxford University Press, 2010). Another helpful resource for understanding our fundamental creatureliness can be found in Kathryn Schifferdecker's *Out of the Whirlwind: Creation Theology in the Book of Job* (Boston: Harvard Divinity School, 2008).

[11] A bull is an official document issued by the pope.

[12] Roger Haydon Mitchell, *Church, Gospel, and Empire: How the Politics of Sovereignty Impregnated the West* (Eugene: Wipf & Stock, 2011), p. 174.

[13] See *C Street: The Fundamentalist Threat to American Democracy* by journalist and best-selling author Jeff Sharlet (New York: Back Bay Books, 2011).

2 The Powers

[1] There are a number of great resources that explore the shape of the principalities and powers, their relationship with the demonic and their role in imperial myths. The classics for this are William Stringfellow's *An Ethic for Christians and Other Aliens in a Strange Land* (Waco: Word Books, 1973); Walter Wink's *Engaging the Powers* (Minneapolis: Fortress, 1992); Rene Girard's *I See Satan Fall Like Lightning* (Maryknoll, NY: Orbis Books, 2001); and Jacques Ellul's *The New Demons* (New York: Seabury, 1975).

[2]John Howard Yoder is one of a number of scholars who make this case. In *The Politics of Jesus* (Grand Rapids: Eerdmans, 1994), p. 137, he argues:

> Something of the same stimulating confusion is present in the thought of the apostle Paul as he applies some of the same thought patterns to different challenges in different contexts. He speaks of "principalities and powers," and of "thrones and dominions," thus using language of political color. But he can also use cosmological language like "angels and archangels," "elements," "heights and depths." Or the language can be religious: "law," "knowledge." Sometimes the reader perceives a parallelism in all these concepts, sometimes not.

[3]Neil Postman, *Amusing Ourselves to Death* (New York: Penguin Books, 1985), pp. vii-viii.
[4]Ellul, *New Demons*, p. 9.

4 Repenting of Christianity
[1]Simone Weil, *On Science, Necessity, and the Love of God* (Oxford: Oxford University Press, 1968), n.p.
[2]For example, I was taught as a teenager never to hug a woman front-to-front, but to give them a "side hug."
[3]Hans Haffner, "Concerning a True Soldier of Christ," *Mennonite Quarterly Review* 5 (1931): 87.
[4]Shusaku Endo, *Silence* (Marlboro, NJ: Taplinger, 1980), p. 171.

5 On the Mysticism of Children
[1]Meister Eckhart, Christmas sermon, quoted in Evelyn Underhill, *Mysticism* (Stilwell, KS: Digireads, 2005), p. 87.
[2]Paulo Freire writes: "Education either functions as an instrument which is used to facilitate integration of the younger generation into the logic of the present system and bring about conformity or it becomes the practice of freedom, the means by which men and women deal critically and creatively with reality and discover how to participate in the transformation of their world." Paulo Freire, *Pedagogy of the Oppressed* (New York: Continuum, 1997), p. 72.
[3]Simone Weil, *Oppression and Liberty* (New York: Routledge Classics, 2001), n.p.
[4]Dorothee Sölle, *The Silent Cry: Mysticism and Resistance* (Minneapolis: Fortress, 2001), p. 13.
[5]Ibid., p. 12.
[6]Freire, *Pedagogy of the Oppressed*, pp. 69-70.
[7]Ignacio Ellacuría, "Discernir el 'signo' de los tiempos," *Diakonia* 17 (1981): 58.
[8]William Stringfellow, *A Private and Public Faith* (Grand Rapids: Eerdmans, 1962), p. 80.

6 Jesus and the Unkingdom
[1]N. T. Wright, "The New Testament and the 'State,'" *Themelios* 16, no. 1 (1990): 11-17.
[2]A special thanks to my friend Jason Evans for teaching me the word "unking" as a way of describing Jesus.
[3]For more on this, see Elisabeth Schüssler Fiorenza, *The Power of the Word: Scripture and the Rhetoric of Empire* (Minneapolis: Fortress, 2007).
[4]David Graeber, *Fragments of an Anarchist Anthropology* (Chicago: Prickly Paradigm, 2004), pp. 3-4.

[5]Ched Myers, "The Fall," in *The Encyclopedia of Religion and Nature* (New York: Continuum, 2005), n.p.

[6]Ibid.

[7]Wes Howard-Brook, *Come Out My People* (Maryknoll, NY: Orbis Books, 2010), p. 196.

[8]This part of Israel's history is particularly troubling. Wes Howard-Brook would argue that such stories are included as propaganda for "Zion theology," which I will address later in this chapter.

[9]Howard-Brook, *Come Out*, p. 95.

[10]Ibid., p. 132.

[11]John Howard Yoder's *The Politics of Jesus* (Grand Rapids: Eerdmans, 1994) does an excellent job of developing this argument.

[12]One of the most helpful books I've encountered that explores the theme of Jubilee in the ministry of Jesus is *The Biblical Jubilee and the Struggle for Life* by Ross and Gloria Kinsler (Maryknoll, NY: Orbis Books, 1999).

[13]I often wonder if any of these folks had babysat him. After all, it is generally assumed that Mary ended up being a single mother at some point, putting more of the parenting burden on Mary. It would suck to have your childhood babysitter try to kill you.

[14]Apologies for my lame anarchist joke. If you don't get it, it is probably for the best.

[15]The whole of Luke's Gospel (and Acts) is so Jubilee-laden that reading it aloud to bankers has the same effect as sunlight on vampires.

[16]Luke 12:13-34 is one of the most compelling economic passages in the entire Bible. I reference it here because many people assume that the call to redistribute wealth to the poor is only made to the rich young ruler in Luke 18. It is a more common theme than that, particularly in Luke's Gospel.

[17]See Wink's *Naming the Powers* (Philadelphia: Fortress, 1984).

[18]Wes Howard-Brook and Anthony Gwyther, *Unveiling Empire: Reading Revelation Then and Now* (Maryknoll, NY: Orbis Books, 1999).

[19]Jacques Ellul, *Anarchy and Christianity* (Grand Rapids: Eerdmans, 1988), p. 88.

[20]See Yoder, *Politics of Jesus*, chapter 10.

[21]Howard-Brook, in Howard-Brook and Gwyther, *Unveiling Empire*, p. 464.

[22]Irenaeus, *Against Heresies* 3.8.1.

[23]Mammon is more than mere "money." It is likely that Jesus (and the early church) thought of mammon as something demonic. "Mammon" not only signified money or wealth but the entire economic system of exploitation. By the Middle Ages, many conceived of mammon as the archdemon of greed.

7 Encountering the Feral God

[1]Dorothee Sölle, *Beyond Mere Obedience* (New York: Pilgrim, 1982), p. 10.

[2]Ibid., pp. 24-25.

[3]It is fashionable for Christians to reject "religion." Often this is largely a semantic game. In this context, I'm not using the word *religion* in a derogatory sense but in the broad way that Wes Howard-Brook defines it, drawing upon the Latin meaning of *religio*, which means to "bind again": "the attitudes, beliefs, and/or practices that bind individuals together as a 'people.'" Wes Howard-Brook, *Come Out My People* (Maryknoll, NY: Orbis Books, 2012), p. 5.

[4]Ibid., p. 7.

[5]Ibid., p. 143.

8 Walking with the Compassionate Christ
[1]Paulo Freire, *Pedagogy of the Oppressed* (Continuum: New York, 1997), pp. 42-43.
[2]Dorothee Sölle, *Suffering* (Philadelphia: Fortress, 1975), p. 36.
[3]Walter Brueggemann, *The Prophetic Imagination* (Minneapolis: Fortress, 2001), pp. 88-89.
[4]Sölle, *Suffering*, p. 164.
[5]I suspect my training to only give "Christian side hugs" may be partly responsible for this.
[6]Lila Watson, United Nations Decade for Women Conference, Nairobi, Kenya, 1985.
[7]Anna of Rotterdam, from "Anna of Rotterdam, Put to Death in That Place, A.D. 1539," in *Martyrs' Mirror*, www.homecomers.org/mirror/martyrs062.htm.

9 Discerning the Subversive Spirit
[1]John Howard Yoder, *Body Politics* (Scottsdale, PA: Herald, 2001), p. 67.

10 Jesus and the Jubilee
[1]See Bruce Levine's *Get Up, Stand Up: Uniting Populists, Energizing the Defeated, and Battling the Corporate Elite* (White River Junction, VT: Chelsea Green, 2011), p. 63.
[2]N. T. Wright, *Jesus and the Victory of God* (Minneapolis: Fortress, 1997), pp. 294-95.

11 Jesus and the Revolutionary Table
[1]Richard Beck, *Unclean: Meditations on Purity, Hospitality, and Morality* (Eugene, OR: Cascade Books, 2011), p. 74.
[2]Ibid., p. 81. Emphasis in the original.

Conclusion
[1]C. S. Lewis, *The Last Battle* (New York: HarperCollins, 1956), p. 196.
[2]David Graeber, *Fragments of an Anarchist Anthropology* (Chicago: Prickly Paradigm, 2004), p. 45.

LIKEWISE. *Go and do.*

....

A man comes across an ancient enemy, beaten and left for dead. He lifts the wounded man onto the back of a donkey and takes him to an inn to tend to the man's recovery. Jesus tells this story and instructs those who are listening to "go and do likewise."

Likewise books explore a compassionate, active faith lived out in real time. When we're skeptical about the status quo, Likewise books challenge us to create culture responsibly. When we're confused about who we are and what we're supposed to be doing, Likewise books help us listen for God's voice. When we're discouraged by the troubled world we've inherited, Likewise books encourage us to hold onto hope.

In this life we will face challenges that demand our response. Likewise books face those challenges with us so we can act on faith.

....

ivpress.com/likewise
twitter.com/likewise_books
facebook.com/likewisebooks
youtube.com/likewisebooks

....